"This is an enormously helpful book for parents struggling with out-of-control kids. Grounded solidly in research, it offers practical and useful advice that can really help parents manage their own emotions and the emotions of their spirited children. It starts by first calming parents and offering a realistic and highly useful plan. Buy this book!"

—**John Gottman, PhD**, author of *Raising an Emotionally Intelligent Child*

"Matis Miller's book is a gift for parents of sensitive, emotional, and sometimes impulsive children. His examples of complicated family life ring true, capturing excruciating dilemmas recognizable to most parents. His well-informed suggestions are compassionate, elegant, and practical. *The Uncontrollable Child* is a deceptively easy-to-read masterpiece that weaves together behavioral theory, dialectical principles, and evidence-based practices from dialectical behavior therapy (DBT) into loving, effective parenting strategies. Miller will help parents survive and solve rigid, polarized parenting traps."

—**Charles Swenson, MD**, psychiatrist in private practice, and associate professor of psychiatry at the University of Massachusetts Medical School

"*The Uncontrollable Child* is an instrumental resource for your parenting reference library. Matis Miller offers clear and thoughtful concepts, and effective navigational tools for some of the most challenging issues in the province of parenting; beautifully illustrating the power of integrating opposites: *acceptance and change*. He reminds us that the greatest gift we can give our child is a healthy parent."

—**Wendy Terrie Behary**, director of The Cognitive Therapy Center of New Jersey and The Schema Therapy Institutes of NJ-NYC and DC; author of *Disarming the Narcissist*; expert; and educator

"Many parents and children struggle with miscommunication, escalating emotions, and struggles around cooperation (or the lack of it). Too often the solutions are to blame someone (sometimes the parent, sometimes the child) and put a lot of work into trying to change the one being blamed. Fortunately, Matis Miller offers a far more useful, and less blaming, approach that balances acceptance and mindfulness with change and learning principles. By understanding these problems as residing primarily in parent-child transactions, he offers a bounty of practical, skill-based interventions largely based on DBT—without judgment or blame. These approaches can be useful for all parents, whether behavior difficulties are ordinary or regularly out of control. Matis provides clear instructions for parents that will be helpful to any family!"

> —**Alan E. Fruzzetti, PhD**, professor of psychology at Harvard
> Medical School, and author of *The High-Conflict Couple*

"Matis Miller's *The Uncontrollable Child* is a uniquely valuable guide to parenting dysregulated children. Given the rise in childhood mood and conduct disorders in recent years, this book provides highly practical, evidence-based strategies that are firmly grounded in a deep understanding of the complex thoughts and beliefs that inform mastering the art of finding the balance between love and limits. I highly recommend this book for all parents."

> —**David Pelcovitz, PhD**, Gwendolyn and Joseph Straus Chair
> in Psychology and Jewish Education at the Azrieli Graduate
> School of Jewish Education and Administration at Yeshiva
> University in New York, NY

"Matis Miller's outstanding *The Uncontrollable Child* brings hope to parents of difficult children. It guides parents in parenting their children with balance and love rather than control and force."

> —**Rabbi Yechiel I. Perr**, president and dean of Derech Ayson
> Rabbinical Seminary in Far Rockaway, NY

"*The Uncontrollable Child* by Matis Miller is a distillation of his mastery of the field and his years of experience into an accessible, easy-to-follow parenting manual for the child who, until now, was seemingly uncontrollable. He empowers parents through a clear and methodical journey to understanding the inner workings of their child, their emotions, and their behavior based on the tenets of DBT—and how to change them."

—**Samuel D. Mandelman, PhD**, developmental psychologist at
the Institute for Cognition and Learning in Brooklyn, NY

The
Uncontrollable
Child

Understand & Manage Your Child's Disruptive Moods *with* Dialectical Behavior Therapy Skills

Matis Miller, LCSW

New Harbinger Publications, Inc.

Publisher's Note

NEW HARBINGER PUBLICATIONS is a
registered trademark of New Harbinger Publications, Inc.

Distributed in Canada by Raincoast Books

Copyright © 2021 by Matis Miller
New Harbinger Publications, Inc.
5674 Shattuck Avenue
Oakland, CA 94609
www.newharbinger.com

Cover design by Sara Christian

Acquired by Jess O'Brien

Edited by Rona Bernstein

All Rights Reserved

Library of Congress Cataloging-in-Publication Data

Names: Miller, Matis, author.
Title: The uncontrollable child : using DBT skills to parent a child with disruptive moods and emotional dysregulation / by Matis Miller, LCSW, ACT, DBT-LBC.
Description: Oakland, CA : New Harbinger Publications, Inc., [2021] | Includes bibliographical references.
Identifiers: LCCN 2020043505 (print) | LCCN 2020043506 (ebook) | ISBN 9781684036868 (trade paperback) | ISBN 9781684036875 (pdf) | ISBN 9781684036882 (epub)
Subjects: LCSH: Problem children--Psychology. | Problem children--Behavior modification. | Child rearing. | Dialectical behavior therapy. | Behavior therapy for children.
Classification: LCC HQ773 .M56 2021 (print) | LCC HQ773 (ebook) | DDC 649/.153--dc23
LC record available at https://lccn.loc.gov/2020043505
LC ebook record available at https://lccn.loc.gov/2020043506

Printed in the United States of America

24   23   22

10   9   8   7   6   5   4   3   2

Contents

Foreword

As President of the Beck Institute, a nonprofit organization that provides training in cognitive behavior therapy (CBT) to mental health professionals worldwide, I am in the enviable position of reviewing dozens of books a year in the mental health field and quite a few about evidence-based practices for children. *The Uncontrollable Child* is an excellent book, one of the best, and its research-based and common-sense approach is, in my opinion, applicable to all children and their caretakers. It is written in an easily accessible, engaging style with numerous examples of what to say and what to do.

Too many books focus too narrowly on the skills parents lack. This book adds essential techniques for parents to use on themselves, to change their own unhelpful beliefs and actions, to reduce their frustration, anxiety, sadness, or sense of inadequacy, so they can be more effective with their kids. Miller vividly describes why learning parenting skills alone isn't enough. Parents often need to change their unrealistic ideas and hopes for their children and move to accepting their child's struggles and difficulties. Practicing the acceptance and mindfulness strategies outlined in this book is a necessary precursor if parents wish to become effective in shaping their children's behavior. Acceptance, realistic expectations, and a calm demeanor are necessary ingredients for change—but difficult to attain without specific guidance.

Miller then provides a clear roadmap for approaching children in a different way. The first step, validation, is crucially important, yet many parents, especially when they're upset, fail to use this strategy. The book offers numerous examples to illustrate precisely how to use validation in a variety of situations. Next, reinforcement strategies are described, followed by specific techniques to reduce unwanted behavior. Setting limits is another essential skill, and the book describes valuable tools for how to implement limits—and equally important, to maintain limits over time. Finally, parents are guided in what to do when others in the family and in the child's environment resist working together to implement the recommendations in the book.

I truly believe that *The Uncontrollable Child*, with its treasure trove of valuable skills, has the potential to help countless struggling parents and their children improve their communication, restore peace to their homes, and pave the way to an optimistic future. It has the potential to make a very significant difference in your family's life—and in your own. Read it, try it, and watch yourself change!

—Judith S. Beck, Ph.D.
President, Beck Institute for Cognitive Behavior
Therapy
Clinical Professor of Psychology in Psychiatry,
University of Pennsylvania

Introduction

I've met countless frustrated parents—clients, friends, lecture audiences—who express a common wish:

If only this child came with a manual!

Parents—even those whose children are not particularly challenging—often find themselves floundering when parenting their children. It would be so much easier, they lament, if they had clear, step-by-step instructions on how to react and respond to everyday parenting situations.

The trouble isn't a lack of information. As a matter of fact, as a parent in the modern world, you have instantly available access to more parenting information than ever before. There are books, lectures, podcasts, websites... You can even get handy bite-sized tips delivered daily to your email inbox.

But sometimes, having all of that information can get confusing. One technique contradicts another. What worked for your first child doesn't work for the next one. You're conflicted about strategies that are so different from those that your parents used.

Don't get stuck on the "tricks that every parent must know" or "the ONE parenting technique that will change your life." When you read *The Uncontrollable Child*, you'll learn that you don't need to choose the "right" way to parent.

This book may not be the be-all-end-all parenting manual (because, realistically, that's impossible), but it's pretty close—and it will give you the perspective and knowledge you need to maximize all of your current skills. It will eliminate the need to find that "perfect method" for parenting because it will help you make the most of *every* technique that you have learned and will learn. Plus, it's loaded with practical, relatable, implementable strategies that will help you along your journey.

The Uncontrollable Child is based on the concepts and skills of dialectical behavioral therapy (DBT), a therapeutic model that broadens the mind and worldview. A main goal of DBT is to find your balancing point, which is unquestionably necessary on the parenting tightrope. As you read, you will learn to balance the extremes of parenting: acceptance with change, flexibility with consistency, limits with love. These principles form a framework you can use to improve upon your go-to parenting techniques while learning new techniques. Most importantly, you'll gain an understanding of *why* these techniques work and how to use them for *your* child and *your* personality.

The Purpose of This Book

In my professional life as a therapist—as well as my personal life as a parent—I meet people who struggle in life. Many of their challenges could have been prevented or eased in childhood.

The formative years are critical to the long-term well-being of every person. The relationships, habits, belief systems, and life skills that are established during childhood and adolescence are the basis of a person's future. The impact of a healthy childhood can last a lifetime, with far-reaching and long-lasting effects.

The Uncontrollable Child is based on the concept that strategic, effective parenting is crucial for a child's long-term success. Parents are one of the most (if not *the* most) influential forces in their children's lives; when you change, your child changes. The purpose of this book is to empower parents to revolutionize their parenting and achieve their goals: to increase their child's positive behaviors; ensure that he feels loved, accepted, and understood; *and* decrease his noncompliant, disruptive, and aggressive behaviors.

Is This Book for You?

DBT and the concepts outlined in *The Uncontrollable Child* are highly effective for children who struggle with impulse control and emotion regulation (i.e., effectively managing and responding to their emotions). These children may or may not have been formally diagnosed with a disorder such as attention-deficit/hyperactivity disorder (ADHD), oppositional defiant disorder (ODD), or disruptive mood dysregulation disorder (DMDD). If your child has one of these disorders or symptoms of any of them (which you'll learn about in chapter 1), this book will help you understand and parent him or her effectively.

Of course, your child doesn't need to have a diagnosis or display particularly challenging behavior to benefit from this book. While *The Uncontrollable Child* is geared toward parents of children with challenging behavior, it isn't only for "uncontrollable children"—it's a guidebook designed to help every parent reach his or her parenting potential.

Climbing the Parenting Mountain

I like to compare parenting to mountain climbing.

Mountain climbing requires skill, knowledge, and tools. Without tools, it's virtually impossible to reach the top. Effective climbers use tools that are designed specifically for varying terrains and applications. Some tools are effective in one situation and not another, while others may be adapted for use in various circumstances. Overusing or underusing a tool may impede the climber's progress. Using the wrong tool at the wrong time can get in the way of reaching the summit, or even cause a backslide.

And, of course, balance is paramount.

Likewise, parenting is a journey that requires special tools. You may already have many tools in your toolbox. However, you may not be using them properly, or you may have a hard time choosing your tool. Perhaps you abandoned a useful tool out of frustration when it didn't work as promised. Or maybe you've never gotten those tools in the first place!

Parenting a child who struggles with emotion regulation requires a special set of tools. Whether you're just starting the climb with a couple of tools or have acquired a set over the years, you'll benefit from a well-organized toolbox and instructions on how to use it. This book provides you with valuable, multiterrain tools that may be adapted to nearly every situation as well as guidance for using them properly.

If you find yourself needing help to use your tools effectively, keep in mind that most expert mountain climbers are not self-taught. There's no shame in seeking out professional assistance (or the advice of other seasoned parents) to help you scale your mountain. If you're already working with a therapist, you can use and discuss the contents of this book alongside and in conjunction with therapy. For less formal support, try reading and reviewing it with a friend who's in the same boat.

In parenting, and in DBT, a healthy balance is vital. Children need a balance of acceptance (being accepted by their parents) and change (behavior modification) in order to flourish. Every person's balancing point is unique. That balancing point is rarely a straight 50:50, so it's important to find the combination that works for you and your child.

The Uncontrollable Child will help you find your balance.

How to Use This Book

This book is designed to be read sequentially, as the foundational concepts will help you use the later skills more efficiently. As you read and implement the skills, you'll learn what works for you.

At the same time, you can always go back to review and practice earlier skills as the need arises. There are constant ups and downs in parenting, and you'll likely have to revisit different sections throughout your journey. You'll mess up at times, and that's okay—as a matter of fact, it's normal and expected. This book is here to help you bounce back when you hit a setback; it will help you navigate your own thoughts and feelings as you climb the parenting mountain.

I recommend that you read *The Uncontrollable Child* in its entirety, even if you are already familiar with the concepts. You may learn new details that will help you use your existing skills more effectively. I also suggest sharing the book or discussing its contents with your spouse or other significant adults in your child's life for maximum effectiveness.

For your convenience, I've created downloadable overviews that summarize the skills and concepts in each chapter, available at the website for this book, http://www.newharbinger.com/46868. (See the very back of this book for more details.) You can use them to guide and remind you as you read and implement the techniques. On the website you'll also find Roadblock Cards. These cards can serve as reminders of the unhelpful beliefs that can get in the way of implementing the skills in this book—as well as ways to "detour" around them. Additionally, the final chapter contains a comprehensive checklist, also available on the website, that recaps all of the skills. Feel free to use it as you read and whenever you need a refresher.

It is my greatest hope that this book will help you climb your personal parenthood mountain, find your balancing point, and enjoy the breathtaking view from the summit.

CHAPTER 1

Getting Started

Nobody ever said that parenting would be easy.

Virtually every parent knows that children aren't just cuddly, adorable things who always do as they're told.

What you may not have known, no matter how well prepared you were for the challenges of parenthood, was that some children are objectively harder to raise than others. Among those are the "uncontrollable" children, and life with them redefines the parameters of what you thought you knew about parenting. When we compare parenting to mountain climbing, these children are the rock faces and steep cliffs.

If you glanced at the title of this book and thought, *Yup, that's my kid*, then you know all about parenting these children. If you just picked it up out of morbid fascination and thought, *Whew, my kid isn't uncontrollable*, don't stop now—everything in here can be helpful to you, too.

An uncontrollable child—one who struggles to regulate her emotions appropriately—need not remain "uncontrolled" for the foreseeable future. With the mindset, framework, and tools that make up dialectical behavioral therapy (DBT), you can once again take control of your parenting.

In this chapter, you'll learn fundamental concepts that will prepare you to understand and implement the information and strategies in the rest of the book. First, we'll examine the hallmarks of uncontrollable children and the unique challenges—and strengths—of this particular personality trait. Next, we'll explore the basics of DBT, starting with the mystery of what, exactly, "dialectical" means and covering the foundational concepts of DBT. And finally, you'll meet a couple of children who may uncannily remind you of certain people living in your household.

Who Is the Uncontrollable Child?

This child is out of control!

She can't handle it when anything goes wrong.

No matter what I do, he just doesn't cooperate.

She refuses to listen to anything I say!

I just can't get through to this kid.

It's a constant battle with him.

Why is she so sensitive about everything?

I can't seem to do anything right with her!

There is no singular definition, no clear-cut description of an uncontrollable child. He takes many forms: the drop-of-a-hat crier, the too-old-for-this tantrumer, the always-on-edge teen, the impulsive wall puncher, the exaggerated drama queen.

Put simply, the uncontrollable child is one who struggles with *emotion regulation*.

Everyone runs into challenges, disappointments, and upsetting moments in life. Most of us are able to regulate our emotions and handle these situations appropriately; sometimes our emotions get the better of us. Uncontrollable children—those who suffer from *emotion dysregulation*—tend to get overwhelmed by their emotions at an above-average frequency. They overreact in ways that are not age-appropriate or socially acceptable: bursts of anger, bouts of sadness, screaming, fighting, even self-harm.

Diagnosing the Uncontrollable Child

Some parents have a hard time seeking a diagnosis for their child. They may prefer not to label him, believe that he'll grow out of it, be afraid of stigma, or feel like something is wrong with them if their child has an "official" disorder.

As a mental health professional, I believe that a diagnosis—technically a cluster of symptoms—can be helpful to determine the proper course of treatment for a child or find an appropriate therapist. It gives a name to your child's symptoms for improved communication between professionals.

Having a diagnosis can make it easier to modify school assignments or adapt your parenting strategies. Additionally, when people have a diagnosis for themselves or their child, it can be very validating; their experiences and challenges suddenly make sense. *I thought I was going crazy, but it turns out that this is something that actually has a name!*

However, depending on the circumstances, a diagnostic label may not be necessary for a child's success. A diagnosis is not an all-inclusive definition of the child, and not every part of her personality can be explained away by a diagnosis. It's not to be used as an excuse or to lead to despair: *I can't do my homework all by myself; I have ADHD!* or *I'll never be able to get her under control; even the psychiatrist said that she has a real diagnosis.* A diagnosis tells us what she *has*—not who she *is*.

Life is challenging when you're struggling with an uncontrollable child. It's important—for your child's well-being and your own sake—to seek help when symptoms are extreme or interfere with her functioning. Let's take a look at some disorders that feature emotion dysregulation: attention-deficit/hyperactivity disorder, oppositional defiant disorder, and disruptive mood dysregulation disorder. Hopefully, this will help you make sense of what's going on with your child and your family.

Attention-Deficit/Hyperactivity Disorder

Attention-deficit/hyperactivity disorder (ADHD) is a fairly well-known disorder that is primarily characterized by inattention, hyperactivity, and impulsive behavior. The symptoms are present before the age of twelve; in some children, they are noticeable from an early age. ADHD can be mild, moderate, or severe.

Symptoms of ADHD include:

- Trouble focusing on tasks and paying attention to detail
- Difficulty following through and completing tasks
- Difficulty organizing activities or keeping track of belongings
- Distractibility or forgetfulness
- Constant motion or difficulty staying still
- Excessive talking and interrupting
- Difficulty waiting one's turn

While most healthy children are impulsive and active, the more extreme characteristics of ADHD significantly impact a child's functioning.

Oppositional Defiant Disorder

Children who are persistently defiant, irritable, angry, argumentative, or uncooperative may be diagnosed with oppositional defiant disorder (ODD).

Symptoms of ODD include:

- Defiant, noncompliant, argumentative, hostile behavior

- Tendency to deliberately upset or annoy others

- Frequent blaming of others for misbehavior

- Vindictiveness or spitefulness

- Frequent irritable and angry moods

- Constant loss of temper

If these symptoms are present for at least six months, the child may qualify for a diagnosis of ODD.

Disruptive Mood Dysregulation Disorder

A newer diagnosis called disruptive mood dysregulation disorder (DMDD) shares several hallmarks with other emotion regulation disorders but has unique features.

Due to its fairly recent addition to the *Diagnostic and Statistical Manual of Mental Disorders, 5th Edition* (DSM-5; American Psychiatric Association 2013), a psychological dictionary of sorts, support for parents of children with DMDD is still developing.

DMDD is diagnosed in children between ages six and eighteen and is characterized by:

- Frequent, recurrent anger outbursts or explosive rages three or more times per week

- Outbursts that are not developmentally appropriate or are out of proportion to the situation

- Chronic, severe, unexplained irritability displayed most of the day, nearly every day, in different settings, lasting for a year or longer

- Symptoms that appear before age ten

- Symptoms that are present in at least two settings (home, school, and/ or with peers)

Prior to 2013, children who displayed these symptoms were often diagnosed with childhood bipolar disorder, which is characterized by severe outbursts and rapidly changing moods. However, when these children were monitored into adulthood, researchers found that their symptoms did not develop into bipolar disorder, meaning they did not have manic episodes or periods of mania and depression. Most went on to experience depression and anxiety as adults, prompting researchers to differentiate DMDD as a new disorder (National Institute of Mental Health 2016).

Because of their heightened emotional sensitivity, children with DMDD are more reactive to negative events and emotions. Their anger outbursts last longer than typical temper tantrums and often reflect a steady level of emotional distress—not just anger—throughout the episode.

The characteristics of DMDD closely resemble those of a disorder diagnosed in adults called borderline personality disorder: emotional dysregulation, intense anger, interpersonal chaos, anxiety, black-and-white thinking, and impulsivity. Because of the similarities between these disorders, DBT, which was originally developed to treat borderline personality disorder, has been found to be particularly effective for children with DMDD. In my professional opinion, DBT is the best course of therapy for these children.

If you are searching for insight into your child's behaviors, you may find a lack of appropriate parenting and therapeutic resources. This is especially likely if your child has a less common diagnosis or no diagnosis at all. That's why I've written this book: to make DBT accessible to the parents of all "uncontrollable" children.

The typical course of treatment for a child with DMDD includes parent training, individual and/or family therapy, and medication in some cases. The goal of DMDD treatment is to teach children to recognize and regulate their emotions, tolerate distress, and develop effective interpersonal skills, all of which are key features of DBT.

Life with an Uncontrollable Child

Parenting an uncontrollable child can be exhausting, frustrating, chaotic, embarrassing, painful, and frightening.

(It's pretty tough on the kid, too!)

It can also come along with a heaping dose of guilt: *What did I do wrong that my child turned out like this?*

Even the most experienced, knowledgeable, patient, loving parents can find themselves with an uncontrollable child: a child who is emotionally sensitive, easily dysregulated, overly moody, or highly irritable.

Emotion dysregulation is often misunderstood, especially by outsiders: *He just needs firm discipline! All she needs is some love! Why can't you get your kid to pull himself together? You must be coddling her; you shouldn't stand for this behavior.*

There's often nothing that the parents could have done to prevent the uncontrollability—most of these children are hard wired to be extra-sensitive, impulsive, or otherwise "uncontrollable." The good news is that there's plenty you can do now to get your life (and your child's life) under control.

As a parent, you have the power to influence your children's lives and enable them to achieve the healthiest state possible. Childhood is the time to accept your child, build him up, protect him, defend him, and love him unconditionally, while simultaneously setting healthy limits, encouraging independence, and teaching him personal responsibility. It's the time to teach him how to deal with emotional struggles on his own, and also the time to teach him how to reach out for help.

The "parent training" component of treatment for children with emotion dysregulation is an essential element. Time after time, I've seen that it's far more effective to encourage parents to change than to encourage children to change. That's because adults generally have a broader worldview than their naturally self-centered children; they're also typically more motivated, more willing to cooperate, and more capable of self-driven change than children are.

This book is not about changing your child: it's about changing your parenting. As you read, you'll learn that changing your parenting is, in fact, a key to behavior change in your children. Effective parenting is crucial for a child's emotional health, and this book will empower you to parent your out-of-control child confidently and appropriately.

The Basics of DBT

Before we get to the skills and strategies in this book, we'll cover the key terms and principles of DBT. Knowing these concepts will help you get into the right frame of mind to learn. It will change the way you think, talk, and act in general, which will affect the way you think, talk, and act with your children.

DBT is a subset of cognitive behavioral therapy (a structured, goal-oriented, evidence-based psychotherapy that addresses cognition, emotion, and behavior). It was developed in the 1980s by psychologist Marsha M. Linehan. While

DBT was originally created to help people with borderline personality disorder who struggle with emotional and behavioral dysregulation (Linehan 1993), it has since evolved. Today, DBT is considered one of the leading methods for treating people with various mood and psychological disorders, and its concepts are useful even for those who do not have any diagnosis. Everyone—especially parents—can benefit from the skills, which help one form healthy, stable relationships and a strong sense of self.

What Does Dialectical Mean?

As you may have guessed, the very essence of DBT is the concept of dialectics, which is woven into the skills and principles that you will learn. Don't be scared off by the word—it's not as scientific as it sounds!

The word "dialectical," which shares a root with "dialogue," is defined as the ability to create a synthesis—a fusion—of two ideas that are (or appear to be) opposite or contradictory. In simpler terms, it's the art of finding the middle ground through dialogue and discussion.

Many experts focus on parenting with love and acceptance *or* on implementing behavioral change and disciplinary strategies. These two approaches may seem to be contradictory on the surface, and parents tend to choose one over the other at various points of the parenting journey. They may focus on acceptance: *Unconditional acceptance will result in a beloved, emotionally healthy child, and I don't want her to think that I'm unhappy with the way she is.* Or they may focus on change: *He needs to learn how to behave appropriately, and all the acceptance and love in the world won't change him.*

However, both acceptance *and* change are necessary for raising healthy, well-behaved, balanced children. An extreme focus on acceptance generally doesn't result in improved behavior; children won't "pick up" appropriate behavior on their own. Similarly, focusing only on change—especially for emotionally sensitive children—typically leads to children feeling misunderstood, defensive, and distressed.

With DBT-based parenting, we recognize the value of both acceptance and change. In this book, you'll learn how to seamlessly implement them at the same time: *I accept and applaud my child for who she is and what she has accomplished,* and *I want to change her current behaviors.*

Try picking up an item with one finger. It's a whole lot easier to pick it up with two, isn't it? You need two fingers, putting pressure on the object from opposite directions, to get a firm grip.

That's the foundation of dialectics: two "fingers" are better than one. While two concepts are (or seem to be) contradictory, you can use dialectics to fuse them together and create a stronger, firmer, more effective approach to parenting.

Why Dialectics?

Acting and thinking dialectically helps us get unstuck: from unhealthy thoughts, from ineffective strategies, from power struggles. With dialectics, there's no "right" or "wrong" method, no black-and-white thinking, no "my way versus your way." Instead, we focus on finding that golden middle path.

The benefits of dialectics are varied. When you start thinking dialectically, you can:

- Expand your thoughts and points of view to include and understand those of your children

- Gain understanding and wisdom into your children's motivation and mindset

- Learn to "unstick" standoffs, resolve conflict with your children, and reduce power struggles

- Decrease isolation, tension, and polarities within yourself and your family

- Become more flexible and approachable for a communicative, close-knit parent-child relationship

- Avoid assumptions and blame, which, in turn, reduces friction and strengthens your bonds with your children

- Learn to balance extremes for effective communication and problem solving

Fundamental DBT Concepts

Marsha Linehan (1993) defined three key DBT principles, which are the foundation of this book. They'll help you start thinking dialectically, enabling you to maximize every strategy.

If you find these concepts a bit overwhelming, don't worry—you don't have to master them before reading the rest of the book. This is just a preview to introduce you to the principles and language of DBT. You'll notice these themes running through each chapter, where you'll learn them in clear, applicable ways. You can always refer back to this chapter as needed.

Concept #1: The world is filled with opposing forces.

Because the very basis of dialectics is the act of reconciling two opposing ideas, this core concept is vital.

The world is a place of opposites. There's matter and antimatter, backward and forward, black and white…and opposites can be true at the same time. You can accept your situation *and* work to change it. You can be tough *and* gentle. You can be doing the best you can *and* need to try harder.

With that in mind, recognize that every side has truth, validity, and legitimacy. There is no singular, undisputed, absolute truth in the physical realm. Our goal is to find the sweet spot, the meeting place, the fusion of two opposing points of view.

"Dialectic" isn't a fancy word for "compromise." Rather, it's the act of recognizing and acknowledging the truth of the other side. It's easy to recognize the truth of your own opinion. The hard part is finding the truth in others' standpoints and identifying the truth that is missing from yours. You achieve dialectical balance when you bring all truths together to create a more complete truth.

To get started down the path of thinking and acting dialectically, try incorporating some of these tips and strategies into your daily interactions:

- Practice looking at all sides and points of view in various situations. Ask yourself: *What am I missing here? What's the "kernel of truth" in their viewpoint?* It may feel like playing devil's advocate.

- Honor and validate the truth on both sides (you'll learn all about this in chapter 5). This does not mean that you're giving up on your values, selling out, or compromising. If you're having a hard time reconciling opposing truths, that's okay—it takes time and practice to train yourself to think differently. Embrace the paradox and become comfortable with it, because the world is filled with opposites.

- Don't focus on right or wrong, good or bad. There is virtually no parenting strategy (short of abusive or neglectful behavior) that is always the "right" or "wrong" way. Instead, focus on being effective and doing what works. (We'll cover this in chapters 3 and 4.)

- Recognize that there's always more than one way to look at a problem. Imagine a giant number written on the ground. From one viewpoint, it's a 6; from the opposite viewpoint, it's a 9. People standing on either side can accurately insist that their viewpoint is the correct one. Try to see that other side, no matter how clear the "right" answer seems to you.

- Adjust your vocabulary. Switch from "but" to "and." As you'll learn in chapter 5, the word "but" cancels out the first part of any sentence. *He's a great kid, but he can't control himself. She's so smart, but she doesn't apply herself to her schoolwork.* Try using "and" in those sentences instead of "but" and you'll see the difference!

- Skip "shoulds." We'll get into this in depth in chapters 2 and 4. The word "should" leads to blaming and assumptions: *She should know better than that. He should not be acting this way.* Instead of dwelling on the way things "should" be, focus on the way they are—and the way they can be.

- Move away from extremes. DBT is most helpful for people who tend to think in extremes, like your black-and-white "uncontrollable" child probably does. Too much or too little of anything can be detrimental. Words like "always" or "never" are considered extremes, so avoid them whenever possible; try using "sometimes" or "often" instead. (However, don't be extreme in avoiding extremes! Sometimes an extreme stance is necessary to help you move away from the other extreme and land in the middle.)

Concept #2: Change is the only constant.

The basic dialectical balance that we strive to achieve in DBT is that of acceptance and change. While positive change may seem impossible at times, especially to parents of challenging children, it's important to remember that the world is constantly changing.

In fact, change itself is the only constant in life. Can you stand in the Mississippi River twice? Sure you can—but it will be different, even if you stand in exactly the same spot, because the river is constantly flowing, shifting, changing.

Whether you're stuck in a moment or a mindset, remember: change is continual, ongoing, and inevitable. We're all older than we were yesterday; you're not the same person you were a moment ago.

Our children change, too, and not just physically. They (and we) change through experience and learning. Even if it may seem that your middle schooler is still struggling with the same behavioral issues she's faced since kindergarten, she's different now that she was then. Thus, the rules—and the strategies you'll use to parent her—will change accordingly.

This concept can be comforting when your child is going through a particularly difficult, annoying, or nerve-wracking stage. She's gone through all sorts of stages in the past that seemed interminable at the time and are now a distant memory. (You may even look back fondly at those times!) Ask yourself: *At age 30, will my child likely still be afraid of the boogeyman, refuse to eat anything but macaroni, freak out in a thunderstorm, or think that potty jokes are the height of hilarity?* The answer is probably (hopefully) no, thanks to the constancy of change. That doesn't mean that you cannot or should not try to address the issue at hand, but remember that it will probably not last forever.

Just as people change, meaning and truth evolve over time as well. Those truths that you may have come to terms with can change with the passing of every moment. Even when we wish they were different, there are times when we need to accept the inevitability of change. (You'll learn how to do that in chapter 3.)

When we adopt the perspective that change is constant, it helps us go with the flow and approach life with flexibility. We develop a comfortable relationship with change so that we can tolerate new challenges and obstacles. It builds resilience to the inevitable unpleasantries of life.

You can incorporate this concept into your everyday life with these strategies:

- Embrace change as it happens. Allow change to happen while acknowledging that it can be hard. As you'll learn in later chapters, embracing the change doesn't mean that you approve, that you want it to happen, or that you are giving up your goals or values.

- Practice fully accepting change, even (especially) when you don't want to. (You'll learn how to do this in chapter 3.) To build up to that point, start small: Take a different route to work. Sit in a different seat. Eat something new for breakfast.

- Don't fight the change that comes with your child's growth. You don't have to like the fact that your child has become a surly teen overnight; remember, it will pass. Embrace it and roll with it in the present instead of lamenting the loss of your adoring and adorable toddler.

Concept #3: Change is transactional.

The third core concept of this book is that change generates change. Every person has different qualities and a unique point of view; at the same time, we're all connected. This connection means that we influence one another in all of our encounters, or transactions, whether intentionally or not.

This is an important truth in all interpersonal relationships, and especially in parenting. A harsh, critical person is likely to receive the same treatment in return; a kind, respectful person will usually see her behavior reflected back from others. You reap what you sow.

Along those lines, when you change, others around you will change in response. You can't change other people, but you *can* change yourself and influence the environment and the people around you.

That's the purpose of this book: to help parents change themselves and their parenting in order to influence their children's behavior. By changing how you think, feel, and act toward your child, you can affect your child's thoughts, feelings, and actions toward you.

You've probably noticed this phenomenon in your other relationships. An extreme stance can push another person to the opposite extreme, commonly seen as "pushback": state an opinion and you're virtually guaranteed to find someone who responds with the opposite view. "Taking mini vacations from your children is essential!" leads to the response, "You should *never* leave your children; they can't feel like anything is more important than them."

To help you put this third concept into practice, keep the following pointers in mind; you'll come across them in various ways throughout the book:

- Pay attention to your effect on others as well as how others affect you. Being able to recognize those effects can help you get to the root of issues and facilitate problem solving. When you observe your child's reactions to your current parenting techniques and interactions, you'll learn what's effective and what's not.

- Look for causes. Everything has a cause—which may be environmental, physical, situational, interpersonal, hormonal, or emotional—and finding that cause will help you determine the most effective course of action. It can be a huge relief to recognize that there is something causing your child's behavior, especially when the behavior doesn't seem to make sense. Finding the cause can make sense of the "nonsensical." And even if you can't find a cause, it can be comforting to know that there *is* a cause.

- Practice letting go of blame (we'll get to that in chapters 3 and 4). It's easy to blame or judge, but this will stand in the way of effective parenting.

Have You Seen These Children?

If you have an uncontrollable child, you may recognize one (or both) of these children:

Meet Lily.

She's a creative, intelligent, seven-year-old social butterfly, the second of three children. She's well loved by her many friends, a natural leader who's constantly surrounded by other kids. Her teachers say that she's an angel at school and genuinely praise her excellent grades, in-class conduct, and above-average social aptitude.

Their only concern is that she gets quiet, withdrawn, and even tearful from time to time, and they're not sure what causes it. At times she can be shy, which seems to be incompatible with her personality. They're not overly worried because she's performing beautifully overall.

Her parents leave parent-teacher conferences wondering if they're talking about the same child.

At home, Lily is a reembodiment of Dr. Jekyll/Mr. Hyde, with too-frequent visits from Mr. Hyde. When things are going well, her family enjoys time with "school Lily": giggly, smiley, great company. But when something sets her off—and that "something" can be anything from a broken pencil to a broken promise—she morphs into a screaming, tantruming, sulking terror.

Needless to say, home is not a pleasant place to be when things don't go Lily's way.

Lily's frustrated parents describe her as overly sensitive. They love her and are troubled by her strong emotions. While they try to accept her for who she is, they understandably have trouble dealing with her outbursts and the ensuing household stress.

The entire family, including Lily's older sister and younger brother, often walks on eggshells to avoid triggering her. However, it's virtually impossible to foresee every trigger. On occasion, her erratic moods have ruined family gatherings, trips, and birthday parties—even her own! It seems like anything can send her into a tailspin: an unexpected change in schedule, a rough day at school, a "no" from her parents, a spat with her siblings, a toy that stops working.

The outbursts are unpredictable and long-lasting; it takes her more time than the average child to get back to herself.

Lily's emotions rise to the surface in the form of high-octane outbursts, complete with crying, yelling, and verbal assaults on her family members. When upset, she often refuses to follow her parents' directives, complains about the unfairness of her life, and tells her parents that she hates them, that she wishes they would die, that they only care about the other kids and don't love her at all. She shuts down and seems unable to listen to—or even hear—attempts to reason with her.

When she gets really out of control, she resorts to pulling her own hair and scratching herself, much to her parents' alarm; they surrender to her demands just to make her stop.

In addition to her tantrums, Lily tends to worry. She struggles with anxiety and constantly asks questions about far-fetched situations that "could" someday happen. "I'm scared that a robber will come in and steal our stuff." "What if a kidnapper takes me?" "What will happen if lightning hits our house and it burns down?" Her parents' patient and reassuring responses never seem to satisfy her. Her mom and dad have cut down on their own date nights because of Lily's fearfulness: she interrogates them about where they're going, how long they'll be gone, who they're going with, and who will be watching her, and she calls them every few minutes while they're out.

Lily's parents are irritated, discouraged, stressed, and anxious, trying to figure out the best way to parent their highly sensitive child.

Then there's Tyler.

Tyler's parents, like Lily's, are at a loss.

The thirteen-year-old has contributed to many of the ups and downs— mostly the downs—of his family's life. He was diagnosed with ADHD at age eight and started taking medication to help with his impulsivity when he was ten. He's seen several therapists, all of whom have helped him in different ways, yet he still struggles with impulse control and other hallmarks of the disorder.

Tyler has a couple of good friends and many strengths, including a knack for anything mechanical; he has become the family fix-it man. For years, he was the classic class clown, but now his terrific sense of humor has matured. His witty, on-the-mark comments always elicit laughs and defuse tension.

Unlike Lily, Tyler is a less-than-stellar student. He struggles with several subjects and has gotten into trouble for fighting. Before he started his ADHD medication, school was a constant struggle—both socially and academically—but with the right dosage and social skills therapy, he's come a long way and is doing fairly well in school.

His home life is a different story.

Late in the afternoon, when Tyler's medication begins to wear off, he has enormous difficulty regulating his impulsivity and his emotions. When he's irritable—which is often—he swears, throws things, slams doors, and becomes physically aggressive to his parents and his brother. He's moody, defiant, and noncompliant, refusing to turn off his gaming system, get ready for bed, do his homework, or come home on time.

Tyler's rages are fracturing his home, literally and figuratively. The holes in the walls, broken hinges, and topsy-turvy bedroom are evidence of his anger. His eight-year-old brother, Alex, is terrified of him, and for good reason: Tyler has hurt him in the past, and his parents feel helplessly unable to protect their younger son. Alex retreats to his room in tears when Tyler becomes aggressive, even when the aggression is not aimed at him. Every family dinner and outing is fraught with tension, often ending in disaster, which deeply affects Alex's sense of security.

Like Lily, Tyler reacts strongly to situations that don't seem to warrant such responses. If Alex gets more ice cream than he does, if his parents aren't available to drive him to the mall, if his expectations aren't met exactly to his standards, if he can't get the latest gadget, if his parents take Alex's side in an argument…Tyler flies off the handle.

His mom and dad—especially Mom, who's a preschool teacher— thought that they knew how to deal with kids like Tyler. But as they operate in survival mode, torn between the needs of their two children, they feel inadequate and resentful. They're too exhausted by the everyday drama and catastrophes, which have been ongoing for years, to appreciate any of Tyler's strengths.

You'll meet Lily and Tyler again at the end of this book, and many similar kids—and their parents—throughout the chapters.

If you can't relate to these examples or if your child is only a "Lily" or "Tyler" once in a while, don't stop reading here! Even parents of run-of-the-mill "controllable" children will learn valuable skills that will enhance and improve their parenting.

The Bright Side of "Uncontrollable"

There's no denying that parenting an emotionally dysregulated child is a challenge. Like every challenge, though, there is often a silver lining. While parenting an uncontrollable child can be incredibly difficult, there are often extraordinary advantages to this personality type: out-of-the-box thinking, drive, passion, resilience, and persistence. Embrace these children and nurture them; you have the ability to help them harness their strengths and shape their future.

Here's a heartening study (analyzed by Suomi 2005) to show you the power of parents. Researchers Krasnegor, Blass, and Hofer (1987) showed that approximately 5 to 10% of rhesus monkeys are more impulsive and/or aggressive than normal. The researchers assigned these biologically "uncontrollable monkeys" to two types of foster mothers: typical mothers and highly nurturing mothers. The monkeys who were raised by the highly nurturing mothers—caring, sensitive mothers who showed their babies affection even during frustrating episodes—grew up to be far healthier than their counterparts. They flourished, faring better than the rest of the monkeys—even the nonaggressive monkeys!

Now that you've learned the fundamentals of DBT—what it is, how it helps, and its basic concepts and themes—you're ready to start applying them to your parenting. As a reminder, you can find an overview of this chapter (and all the other chapters) at http://www.newharbinger.com/46868. You'll encounter these concepts as you journey through the skills and strategies that we'll cover in the next eight chapters, starting with the basics of acceptance in chapter 2.

Your parenting mountain may be an unforgiving one, but remember that scaling Mount Everest is a remarkable feat. The climb is difficult, but reaching the top will bring you the greatest sense of satisfaction, accomplishment, and fulfillment (not to mention bragging rights)…and the view is just spectacular. So hang in there—you can do this!

Acceptance: The Key to Change

As you walk the road to balanced parenting, you'll encounter countless unexpected twists and turns—pleasant and unpleasant, joyful and sorrowful, satisfying and frustrating. That's why we focus on acceptance first: it smooths the road ahead, empowering you to make effective choices and use your skills successfully, no matter what challenges you may face.

So what does *acceptance* mean in the context of successful parenting?

First, it's not an abstract, intangible concept that's difficult to describe and develop. Rather, acceptance is an active process—it's something you *do*. It has specific tactics and strategies that you can learn and use. And when you move toward acceptance, it can strengthen your relationship with your child and help you both achieve positive change.

In this chapter, you'll learn:

- The definition of acceptance that we'll use in this book

- The purpose of acceptance in the context of parenting a challenging child

- The relationship between acceptance and change

- How acceptance improves our relationships

- How to overcome obstacles to acceptance

Finally, we'll explore the factors that can interfere with acceptance and start building the skills to overcome them so that we can be the parents our kids need us to be.

What Acceptance Is (and Isn't)

Put simply, *acceptance is making peace with reality as it is.* We recognize the facts about both the here and now and the realistic future. When we are in acceptance mode, we don't actively do anything to change the present moment. We just see it clearly and allow it to be what it is.

Maybe this sounds great to you; maybe it sounds like an impossible challenge. It's true that moving toward acceptance can be difficult, but it's doable, through specific, practical measures. It's also key to growing the parenting skills you most need.

Acceptance does not magically make a situation all better or make uncomfortable circumstances disappear. It will not change your child's nature, and it won't change his behavior overnight either. Pain still exists, and it may be intense. Acceptance will simply make it easier to move forward without suffering.

There's a stark difference between *pain* (which is part of life) and *suffering* (which may be avoidable). The difference is acceptance:

Pain + acceptance = pain

Pain + nonacceptance = suffering

Take a moment to picture a story that illustrates this truth. Two young men find themselves imprisoned for crimes they did not commit and are each placed in solitary confinement.

One prisoner begins his sentence bemoaning his fate and wallowing in his devastation. As time goes on, he comes to realize that his situation is unlikely to change anytime soon. He is understandably upset. But he also accepts the fact that he will be spending his days locked up. He begins exploring the limited opportunities offered to him: the prison library, a degree program for incarcerated people, physical exercise, letters to his family. He focuses on self-improvement and connection with the world outside.

His fellow inmate cannot accept the reality of his situation. Even after months, he rages against the unfairness. He paces his cell in a constant state of agitation and fury. He sleeps badly, eats poorly, and can't concentrate on anything but the injustice of his life. He lives in an unbearable state, slowly driving himself into madness.

Both men are in pain. But only one is suffering.

In short: acceptance does not mean that you *want* things to be this way, that you like the situation, that you have chosen this life (consciously or subconsciously), or that you approve of it. It simply means that you're acknowledging and accepting the reality (including the pain and the struggle) as you move through life as effectively as you can.

Acceptance and Change: The Balance

There are countless problems in this world. Yours may be parenting a child with emotional dysregulation; your neighbor may struggle with a difficult marriage; your sister may be chronically unemployed. While every problem is different, there are only four possible ways to deal with a situation that feels like a problem—no matter what that problem is:

1. Solve it.

2. Change how you feel about it.

3. Tolerate it.

4. Stay miserable (or make things worse).

In many situations, you don't have to limit yourself to one option. You can accept a problem and then work toward changing it, or tolerate it while trying to change how you feel about it. In other situations, you may have only one option. But these are the only four possibilities. It's an expanded version of the Mother Goose rhyme:

For every evil under the sun,

There is a remedy, or there is none.

If there be one, try and find it;

If there be none, never mind it.

Option 1: Solve It

Many problems can be solved (though it isn't always easy) by looking for a workable solution. Hungry and irritable? Go get a snack. Not happy with your job? Start looking for a new one. Child's not doing well on her meds? Time for a new psychiatrist.

Finding a solution to your problem is technically a change strategy, though acceptance is often necessary to find that solution. It might seem that acceptance and change are conflicting concepts: if I accept, I'm not changing; if I try to change, then I'm not really accepting! But the truth is that both acceptance and change are necessary, and they can be balanced according to your child's needs and your own.

Before attempting to solve a problem, you need to recognize and accept the reality in order to achieve realistic change. For example, a struggling undergrad student who has barely eked out a single passing grade cannot reasonably hope to be accepted to an Ivy League law school.

That's the importance of acceptance in parenting (and really in every area of life): you can only be effective after you accept the reality of whatever life has handed you. When you acknowledge that your child is emotionally sensitive/ has ADHD/(fill in your challenge here), you can use that information as you chart a path toward change and move forward effectively.

That's the acceptance/change balance: we want to accept the reality *and* do what we can to change it. Once you accept and tolerate your situation as it is, you may discover alternative pathways to change. Your child has an explosive temper? Now that you've come to terms with that, you can move from telling him to "just get your act together" to trying new skills like validating his struggles or giving him space when he's irritable. Your kids' temperaments clash so badly that you can't do anything to change their dynamics? Once you've accepted that, you can work on other solutions—like shuffling their sleeping arrangements or schedules—instead of trying to make them get along.

Remember the prisoners? The one who accepts his reality can't change the reality of his imprisonment, but he is able to move forward with what he has. Once he accepts the fact that he's serving a life sentence (unfairly), he can figure out how to be most effective while he's imprisoned.

Option 2: Change How You Feel About It

Once you've accepted your problem and gotten in touch with reality, you may find that there is no solution at the moment. Instead of focusing on change or a solution, you can adjust your emotional response with skills such as mindfulness and opposite action (we'll get to that in the following chapters).

You can also influence your emotions by adopting a different perspective. Seeing things from a different angle can change your feelings about it. Replace *This kid is giving me such a hard time* with *He must be having a hard time.* Even actions unrelated to the problem itself—like eating better, sleeping more, or exercising—can help you feel better.

The man who's found himself wrongfully imprisoned, for example, cannot change his situation. He can, however, change his attitude toward it. Rather than focusing on the unfairness and unpleasantness of his reality, he can choose to change his outlook: *This is an opportunity for me to focus on myself and become a better person.*

Option 3: Tolerate It

When the situation cannot be changed, learn to tolerate it, meaning accept it unconditionally (which is the focus of this chapter and the next). You may not feel any better about the problem, but you'll feel better about *having* a problem. This is a common reaction to loss; over time, the pain lessens, but it doesn't disappear. It morphs from sharp, stabbing agony to dull aches. Tolerating the pain doesn't change the fact that there *is* pain, but it eliminates the suffering.

We're naturally programmed to *solve problems*: fixing the broken toilet, looking for a new job when we're unhappy with the current one, hiring a tutor to help a struggling child. Unfortunately, while accepting reality can and often does lead to change (as we discussed in option 1), sometimes change is not an option. There are truly unchangeable situations, and no amount of acceptance can change that.

When it comes to parenting, you're likely to encounter many unchangeable factors. Not every aspect of a child is changeable: genetics, temperament, some environmental elements, birth order, even certain deeply rooted behaviors are more or less fixed. When there's no possibility of change, parents must accept those traits and circumstances.

Even when change is an effective or realistic option, you may find that change strategies lose effectiveness over time. What works with one child may not work with another or may stop working as he ages. You may put in countless efforts to help a child—psychotherapy, medication, parent training, mentoring—and see minimal progress.

In all situations, both changeable and unchangeable, acceptance helps us cope with the harsh and painful realities of life.

This is the essence of our prison metaphor: when Prisoner #1 accepts his situation, his suffering lessens, though his pain remains. Sometimes, acceptance leads to change; sometimes it's vital on its own. Even if the acceptance wouldn't lead to change—if he'd decide to simply live each day in prison, without working on bettering himself or his situation—he would live a more peaceful life.

Option 4: Stay Miserable (or Make Things Worse)

Of course, there's also the other prisoner in our story: Prisoner #2, who refuses to accept his reality and continues to suffer. Nonacceptance, or fighting reality, is also a choice. Prisoner #2 has a very valid reason to feel despondent, but he chooses to remain miserable rather than choosing one of the other three options.

When you choose to stay miserable, you may veer into making things worse: yelling at your kid, sending a nasty text to your boss, eating an entire pint of rocky road. Misery in itself may feel good in the short term; it's easier than acceptance and may get you extra attention and validation. But wallowing in misery causes long-term suffering and additional pain.

When you face an unchangeable reality, focusing exclusively on change may lead to frustration and hurt, which often makes the situation even worse. This can be a difficult reality for parents. We deem our children's behavior "unacceptable" and declare that they "have to change." Then, when we've tried everything and they don't change, we continue to search for that elusive "other option." *Yes, but there has to be another way to fix this behavior! These can't be the only choices!* In reality, there isn't another way (at least not presently). We cannot always "solve" our children.

Have you ever taken a child to a batting cage? You may have encountered this all-too-common scenario: the rookie batter heads straight for the high-speed cage, claiming he's the best hitter in his class. He isn't quite prepared for the rapid-fire pace when the balls start flying. He reacts by standing there, yelling and crying as the balls hit him, demanding a do-over: "It's not fair! I didn't know it would be this fast! Nobody could possibly hit these balls!"

And so many parents react by hollering at their kids, "The balls are coming, just pick up the bat and start hitting, or at least get out of the way!"

As a parent of an "uncontrollable" child, you may not have been prepared for the challenges of parenting. The balls came flying at you at warp speed. You can deny and fight the reality of your life: *I can't take this anymore! I wouldn't have had kids if I'd known how hard it would be! I'm totally overwhelmed! Why can't he just be normal?*

That's fighting reality, and it will make you miserable—and get in the way of effective change. As long as you stay mired in the nonacceptance slump, you won't be able to *do what works.*

Instead, you can recognize and accept the reality: *The balls are coming no matter what. This is my life. What do I do now?*

Once you stop fighting, you can work with what you have in order to achieve change. Acceptance clears a path to more choices: you can take your best swing at effective parenting (option 1), you can work on changing your own feelings about your parenting and your child (option 2), or you can tolerate it: step out of the way and watch the balls fly by, accepting what you thought was unacceptable (option 3). Either way, you'll minimize the pain of being pelted by those balls.

Acceptance Fosters Healthy Relationships

While acceptance is essential in handling our daily lives and challenges, it's also essential for loving relationships. Just as acceptance helps us deal with our problems effectively, it helps us navigate and enhance our relationships. (Similarly, just as nonacceptance makes things worse, it hurts relationships as well.) This includes our relationship with ourselves as well as our parenting relationships.

We'll start with our relationship with ourselves.

We parents are all too often hindered by guilt and a negative outlook on ourselves and our parenting abilities. As a parent in the modern world, you're likely bombarded with images of the "perfect parent" who seems light years away from your own parenting. You may feel judged and guilty for not serving the right foods (*Supermom next door just lectured me about clean eating and how food coloring is giving my kids ADHD*), for yelling at your child (*That article said that even raising your voice once will damage a kid's emotional well-being*), for not sitting down to play endless games of Candyland (*I'm bored to tears, but what if she thinks I don't like spending time with her?*), or for not keeping up with the latest parenting must-do.

And when you're the parent of a more challenging child, the guilt is amplified: *Where did I go wrong? I must be the world's worst parent. How could I have raised a child who acts this way?*

These thoughts are harmful, as they will likely lead to your seeing yourself as a failure for not doing enough or for acting ineffectively. They lead to intense guilt, anxiety, or even depression, which significantly impairs your functioning as a person and as a parent, ultimately impacting your children.

The very fact that you're reading this book indicates that you're doing the best you can *and* that you want to improve. Learning to better accept *yourself* will help you regulate your own emotions, which, in turn, will positively affect *your child*. (Remember, *change is transactional*.)

Acceptance is not always a feel-good exercise; facing the reality of your and your child's less-than-desirable traits can stir up a lot of negative emotions and frustration. Don't worry—that's entirely normal and it's okay to feel those emotions! The acceptance strategies that you'll learn in the next chapters will help you face those thoughts and feelings head-on as you strengthen and maintain your relationship with your child.

For us as parents, acceptance means learning to love and appreciate our children for who they are. We work to understand what makes our children tick so that we can love them for their positive qualities, strengths, and traits, *and* for their quirks, flaws, and idiosyncrasies. Acceptance has the power to change the way we view and relate to our children.

Children can keenly sense whether they are accepted by their parents. When you look at your child and consciously choose to accept her as she is— warts and all—you will feel more love and compassion toward her, and she will feel that love and compassion.

Throughout your child's development, she has several core emotional needs, including the need to feel loved, cared for, understood, accepted, valued, safe, secure, and stable. She also needs to be allowed to express anger and other negative emotions. Children are growing and learning, and it is our job as parents to meet these complex needs as they grow and learn.

If we are consistently negative in our interactions with our children, they can develop negative core beliefs about themselves and the world. These beliefs lead to emotional impairments and a poor ability to cope with stress and emotional pain in adulthood. No parent will perfectly meet every single emotional need of his child. We all do the best we can—*and* we can improve. Even after long periods of negativity, an increase in acceptance and positivity allows children to develop into healthy and happy people.

Acceptance benefits both you and your child. You will form a deeper, healthier attachment and understand her motivation. She will feel your support and connection, which fosters a healthy sense of self-esteem and confidence. She will see that you love her despite—or maybe even because of—her flaws, and learn that she is lovable and valuable.

And there's a bonus: the very process of accepting your child can help create change in him. Many acceptance strategies you'll learn, such as validation (chapter 5), naturally lead to behavior change.

When your child feels loved and accepted unconditionally, it improves his ability to accept himself. This, in turn, helps him regulate his emotions and get himself "unstuck" more easily to work toward change. Additionally, a child who knows he is accepted is more likely to respond positively to limit setting. He is able to understand that your limits are set for his own good—even if he won't admit it or insists otherwise.

The journey to acceptance starts with building a connection with your child. In later chapters you'll find exercises that will help you create that connection. You'll also find self-acceptance strategies for yourself as a parent.

Roadblocks to Acceptance

Of course, there are lots of factors that get in the way of acceptance. In particular, certain beliefs and emotions can—and often do—interfere.

Emotions such as anger, sadness, guilt, shame, and rage can hamper our ability to accept. It's hard to accept when we're in an emotional state because acceptance takes effort. Heightened emotion tends to crowd out rational thinking and effective action.

When strong emotional states take hold of you, allow yourself to feel and accept the emotion. Observe, label, and validate your emotions, and then regulate yourself so that you can move toward acceptance. If you're feeling ashamed about your child's out-of-control behaviors in public, validate yourself (*It makes sense that I'm embarrassed when he acts like that in front of other people*) and allow yourself to feel the shame, letting it come and go. (You'll learn how to do that in the following chapters.)

The emotions that get in the way of acceptance are often rooted in distorted thinking. These "thinking errors" and beliefs lead to heightened emotion—anxiety, fear, guilt, confusion—which often prompts parents to move to an extreme and become rigid and authoritarian. This can lead to the child's feeling unaccepted, misunderstood, and unloved. He may express his self-doubt and struggle to accept himself through behavioral outbursts.

Thinking errors are often deeply ingrained in a parent's parenting style and opinion of her child. One common thinking error is the word "should": *How can I accept it if she shouldn't be doing it in the first place? He should know better! This should not be happening!*

"Should" suggests that you're ignoring or overlooking the cause of the behavior and getting stuck on *what you wish were true* rather than *what actually is true*. This keeps you from working effectively toward a realistic solution. Skip the "shoulds"—harping on the fact that something "should" be a certain way will hamper your ability to make that "should" a reality.

Here are some common thinking-error roadblocks—beliefs that get in the way of your ability to solve, accept, or reframe real problems—and some detours, or tactics for getting around them. These "roadblocks" and "detours" are also available as cards that you can download at http://www.new harbinger.com/46868 (see Chapter 2 Roadblock Cards) and print to use as frequent reminders.

Roadblock (the belief)	Detour (the response)
It's impossible for me to accept the unacceptable.	Think of other times in your life when you've accomplished something you had deemed "impossible." Just because something *feels* impossible doesn't mean it *is* impossible.
If I accept my child's behavior, that means that I'm okay with it.	Remember: acceptance is not synonymous with approval. We can (and frequently do) accept situations that we would prefer not to encounter, such as sitting in traffic or being waylaid by bad weather!
My child needs to realize that I'm the one in charge here! *She can't just act however she wants. If I accept, she will take advantage and manipulate me.*	Ask yourself: Is fighting the reality changing anything? Is she getting the message? When you accept, you're more likely to be able to figure out effective ways to set limits and help your child respond to them. Remember: you can accept your child **and** maintain limits and self-respect!
It's too late for us; the damage is done.	Remember that *change is constant*—it's never too late. Embracing positivity and acceptance shows your child that change is possible and repairs past pain, one small step at a time.
He should know better than this!	Let go of "shoulds." Practice mindfulness to overcome judgment and move toward acceptance.
I'm too upset to deal with this right now!	Take a step back; remove yourself from the situation, use relaxation skills, or distract yourself to become calmer prior to using acceptance skills.

If you can relate strongly to any of these, feel free to come up with your own tactic for modifying the belief. It can help to keep reminders on your phone or written on the front and back of index cards that you keep on hand. For example, you might write the following:

When I think, "I'm in charge! She can't act how she wants!" I can breathe and say instead, "Yes, I'm in charge. And she's acting out. What can I do right now to keep my cool, reinforce the limits, and keep our connection?"

In all areas of acceptance, it's important to remember that you're only human—and that means that you're pretty much guaranteed to mess up sometimes. It's understandable. It's okay. And it's even beneficial for your child!

It's good for children to see that their parents are people, too. They'll see that you have emotions and that you also get frustrated, angry, sad, or emotional. When your child sees that you can handle your emotions, you've modeled everything that you want him to emulate. Actions are more powerful than lectures. And when you *don't* handle emotions effectively, that's also a powerful lesson: parents aren't perfect, and they know how to apologize when they mess up.

Acceptance isn't easy—*and* you can do it. As you now know, its benefits are enormous, especially to parents of "uncontrollable" children. The next three chapters will focus on what you can do—realistically and concretely—to move toward acceptance. Acceptance may seem like an abstract concept, but in reality it is a quantifiable and concrete process. In chapter 3 you'll learn specific acceptance skills, strategies, and helpful mantras to facilitate acceptance. Chapter 4 will cover mindfulness, a necessary skill for acceptance. When you learn and practice mindfulness, it helps you understand your child's behavior, define challenges in parenting, and increase your awareness in order to parent effectively. Chapter 5 will focus on another crucial component of acceptance, validation. When executed properly, validation improves the parent-child relationship, boosts the child's self-esteem, and helps the child regulate his emotions.

CHAPTER 3

Practical Acceptance Strategies

Now that you've read about the importance of acceptance, you may be feeling empowered and ready to be that accepting, patient, tolerant parent you've always wanted to be.

Well…you're definitely on your way, and that's a huge accomplishment—*and* (not but) there's still plenty more to learn.

Although it may feel like a Herculean task now, with practical, concrete acceptance strategies, you can and will find yourself moving toward acceptance—even under the most challenging circumstances.

In this chapter, you'll learn:

- What "radical acceptance" is

- How to practice acceptance in unchangeable situations

- Various how-tos of acceptance

What Is Radical Acceptance?

Accepting reality is an incredibly difficult skill. We tend to seek solutions, to play Mr. Fixit, to try to make it all better. But one of life's harshest realities is that some situations simply cannot be changed—sometimes for a specific period of time, other times indefinitely.

As a parent, those situations may be a child's personality trait or temperament, a diagnosis, a learning disability, sibling rivalry, a less-than-ideal home layout, or even a school rule.

In an unchangeable situation, you can choose to wallow in the wishes and the what-could-have-beens (and remain miserable—remember the four options for dealing with a problem?), or you can work toward complete, total, absolute acceptance, or *radical acceptance* (as it's known in DBT). This type of acceptance takes a huge amount of effort and often initially triggers a lot of pain and sadness.

Once you move past the sadness stage (which tends to be short-lived), you can reach unconditional acceptance, which is extraordinarily liberating.

Imagine that you're in a house that's on fire. You can choose to hunker down in the back room that hasn't been engulfed in flames (yet) and suffer smoke inhalation as you succumb to hopelessness, or you can choose to get out of the house, which requires running through the blaze. Full acceptance may be painful, but it's lifesaving! That brief period of pain and sadness, though it may be intense, is far preferable to the suffering you'll encounter when you remain mired in anger or bitterness.

As we say in DBT, the only way out of hell is through misery.

There are times when you'll think you've accepted something, but resentment or other negative feelings may still be simmering under the surface. Radical acceptance is when you wholly accept the situation (or the child in question) as is and stop fighting reality. It's completely accepting the situation in your heart, your mind, and your body.

Remember: radical acceptance will most likely bring sadness, and that's normal. Accepting does not mean being happy about the circumstances; it's okay to say, *I completely accept this reality even though I wish it were different.*

Now, before you start radically accepting things that are not quite acceptable (*I accept that I'm a terrible parent who can't stop screaming at my kid!* or *My child is just one big screw-up. He'll be like this forever, so I may as well stop trying to help him*), realize this:

Acceptance does not mean giving up.

If you radically accept the fact that your child is highly impulsive despite trying every single medication out there, that doesn't mean that you've accepted that reality forever. If a new medication hits the market in a year from now, you shouldn't forgo a trial because you've resigned yourself to the reality ("I've accepted that this is the way he is, so why should I keep trying?").

Never give up on the possibility of change. Radical acceptance applies to the facts that exist in the present moment (and that are highly probable in the future). As you know, change is constant—so accepting the reality of today does not mean giving up hope for tomorrow.

Acceptance Strategies

Remember your mountain-climbing adventure? When it comes to those everyday parenting moments when your kid has pushed *your very last button*, acceptance can feel as insurmountable as Mount Everest. You may be able to identify the tools that you'll need to scale that mountain, but if you haven't been trained to use them properly, all they'll do is weigh you down.

These concrete, practical strategies can be pulled out of your toolbox during the most challenging times to help you reach the summit:

- Pros and cons

- Connect to accept

- Look for similarities

- Turn your mind

- Willingness vs. willfulness

- Opposite action

- Cope ahead

Let's delve into what these strategies involve.

Pros and Cons

This skill is simple, almost deceptively so, but effective: weigh the pros and cons of a situation, drawing up a clear list so that you can compare and contrast. The pros and cons skill is useful in various areas of parenting and can help you achieve both acceptance and change.

If you're having trouble with acceptance, this skill is a great starting point. You can begin by using it to clearly see and analyze the advantages and disadvantages of acceptance (and yes, there are disadvantages!) and of nonacceptance, which can help you overcome the obstacles that are blocking your path.

You'd think that there aren't any pros of fighting reality, but if your current coping skills (or lack thereof) weren't providing some gain for you, you wouldn't continue using them! Those problematic behaviors do something for you. Fighting the reality may give you some semblance of hope as you struggle to make your child behave like he "should" behave. Acceptance, on the other hand, is facing his limitations and coming to terms with the fact that you will not change who he is. Acceptance can be painful, and it's natural to want to avoid it.

The trouble is, the advantages of nonacceptance are usually short term, while the benefits of acceptance are long term. Short-term effects are very powerful. I always say that drugs and alcohol are an excellent solution to pain and problems: they numb the pain very quickly and effectively, making the user feel better immediately. However, in the long run, the effects are disastrous: addiction, overdoses, health issues, death.

While long-term solutions may be more difficult to implement, they're ultimately more advantageous.

Writing down and evaluating the pros and cons can help you see the broader picture and move forward effectively. Here's how:

Pick a quiet time when you are feeling calm and aren't likely to be interrupted. Draw up a chart detailing the pros and cons of both acceptance and nonacceptance. Then label each pro and con as a long-term (LT) or short-term (ST) effect.

Your charts may look like these:

Pros and Cons of Acceptance

Pros	Cons
• Improves my relationship with my child (LT)	• Can be really difficult! (ST)
• Decreases tension in the house (LT)	• Feels like giving up, giving in, or approving of the situation, even if I know it's not (ST)
• Decreases my stress (ST/LT)	• May get flak from other people for "not disciplining enough" (ST)
• Increases my child's self-esteem (LT)	
• Makes my child feel loved (ST/LT)	• Will likely cause feelings of sadness ("I don't want to give my child medication" or "I never wanted a life like this") (ST)
• Helps me get in touch with reality (ST/LT)	

Pros and Cons of Nonacceptance

Pros	Cons
• Gives me a feeling of control over the situation ("I know that I'm right, and this is simply not okay!") (ST)	• Exhausting and ineffective to constantly fight the reality (ST/LT)
• Shows my child that I disapprove of his behavior (ST)	• Unpleasant environment at home (ST/LT)
• Feels good to stick to my principles (ST)	• Damage to parent-child relationship (LT)
• Don't have to work through difficult emotions in the acceptance process (ST)	• Leaves my child feeling like there's something wrong with him (ST/LT)

Think realistically about the long-term effects. Picture your life in a week from now, in three months, in six months, in a year, in five years…if you would accept reality and if you would not accept it.

Creating these charts takes time and effort (and honesty with yourself), but it's worth it. It will help you examine your reality to find out what is and isn't working for you—and why—so that you can figure out how to act more effectively from now on.

Once you have the skill down pat, you'll be able to apply it to other areas of parenting. You may analyze the pros and cons of your child's personality, of particular therapies or after-school programs, or of your favorite parenting strategies. The possibilities are endless!

Connect to Accept

Sometimes the warm-and-fuzzies of the unconditional parent-child bond can be hard to conjure up, especially with a challenging child. At those times, you may find yourself focusing so much on her demands and difficulties that you lose sight of your connection with her. Take the time to rekindle that connection—and you don't even have to involve your child!

Choose a quiet time to reflect on your child's personality. These questions should get you started:

- What do you love about your child?

- When does your child make you smile?

- What are your child's passions? What does he enjoy?

- What makes her happy? Sad? Angry? Frustrated?

- What scares your child?

- What are your child's good qualities and strengths? What are your child's challenges and the possible causes of those struggles? (Approach this from your child's perspective, not the challenges that he presents in your life.)

- What positive traits have others (friends, relatives, teachers, neighbors, even strangers) attributed to your child? What would you like others to say about your child?

- What potential do you see in your child? In which areas do you see her becoming successful? (That strong-minded, stubborn, argumentative, impulsive, emotionally sensitive child who harnesses her traits may just become a successful lawyer or business owner!)

Make a written list so that you can review it regularly, even daily.

A great time to perform or review this exercise is when your child is asleep. Look at his sweet, uninhibited face, the vulnerable one that you don't get to see when he's awake. It's easiest to see the good in your child and to feel loving toward him when he's silent and far off in dreamland. You'll be much more charitable when he looks like the cherubic baby you brought home from the hospital rather than the demanding, defying, limit-testing rascal who constantly tries your patience!

Not enough? Spend some time flipping through pictures and videos of him at his most adorable moments—even if that delightful toddler is now a less-than-delightful teen. It'll help you connect with him again and become more accepting of all of his traits.

Look for Similarities

Another way to deeply connect with your child is to identify similarities between the two of you. It can be easy to focus on the differences, especially when your kid is particularly difficult (*Where did this kid come from? Not from my side of the family, I know*). Viewing a child as the "black sheep" in your family distances him from you, both in your mind and in his.

Focus on how your child resembles you to help you relate to and accept him. Think about shared experiences, personality traits, preferences, or even physical features. (Focus on the positive here; finding similarities in areas that you don't like about yourself will lead to dangerous territory! If you zero in on the traits that you hate most about yourself and can't bring yourself to accept, that will get in the way of accepting your child.)

Write down at least five similarities—even the "little things," like "She has my cleft chin" or "He likes cinnamon buns better than donuts, just like I do"—to feel more connected to your child. Even if your child seems to be the exact opposite of you, you may surprise yourself with the similarities you uncover!

Turn Your Mind

Remember that acceptance isn't a let's-get-this-over-with one-time event; it's a process, a journey that's often beset by potholes, detours, traffic, and unexpected delays. Consider parenting to be a long road trip: keep the destination in mind, enjoy (or tolerate) the stops along the way, and remember that you'll never get to where you're going if you don't start driving.

Throughout the journey of acceptance, you'll need to *turn your mind* toward acceptance, consciously making the choice to accept the situation at hand. Mindful breathing—purposefully focusing your attention as you naturally inhale and exhale—combined with a short phrase such as "I accept" or "It is what it is" can help you get there. If you're more of a visual thinker, visualize approaching a fork in the road and physically turning onto Acceptance Road.

Because acceptance is a constant process, you'll most likely need to practice turning your mind over and over again at different stages of the journey. Become aware of the thoughts, emotions, and sensations that crop up when you start heading in the wrong direction—that knot in your stomach, the heat in your face, the thought, *This kid is impossible*—so that you can steer back to Acceptance Road before you miss the turnoff altogether.

Willingness vs. Willfulness

Willingness is the act of being effective and doing what's necessary to resolve a situation successfully, even if the reality is painful. *Willfulness* is the opposite of *doing what works*: it's inflexibility, refusal to tolerate reality, fighting for something that's not going to happen. If you've ever seen a kid who refuses to get into the elevator because his sister pushed the button (and it was his turn!), you've seen willfulness in action.

In teens and adults, the tantrums are executed more maturely (or so you hope), but the emotion and thought process are the same. As a parent, you may get mired in willfulness when you stick with a parenting technique even though it's not working (or is making things worse). For example, you may keep giving your child harsher punishments, even though punishment has never helped improve her behavior, because you believe that *this is what she needs, and she'll learn eventually.* (Recognize this line of thinking? It may also sound like this: *This is the way my parents disciplined me; kids today are out of line and need to understand that they can't get away with these behaviors!*)

When you face reality, you reach another fork in the road. You can choose to turn to willfulness and stay stuck and miserable (there are those four ways to handle a problem again), or you can choose to be willing, turn toward acceptance, and do what works.

The first step to moving toward willingness is recognizing when you're being willful. Notice and identify your thoughts and their corresponding emotions: *I can't do this anymore. Enough is enough. I give up on this whole "being a better parent" thing. This is so unfair!* That's the frustration and the willfulness talking. (A willful statement is often a "Yes...but...": *Yes, he's smart, but a little too smart for his own good. Yes, she's doing better socially, but she's still acting up at home. Yes, the psychologist said he has ODD, but I think it's overdiagnosed and he can do better if he just tried.*)

Willfulness may manifest itself physically, too: tensed-up back muscles, feelings of agitation, gritted teeth, clenched hands.

When you notice these thoughts, emotions, and sensations, label them for yourself: *This is willfulness.* Recognizing that you're feeling willful is half the battle. Once you've done that, try to steer toward willingness instead: *I wish things would be different, but they're not. I need to work toward accepting this.*

Just because you're feeling willful doesn't mean you have to act willfully. To physically turn to willingness when you're feeling frustrated or upset, the following exercise will help.

HALF SMILE AND WILLING HANDS

Go to a quiet place. Take a deep breath. As you think about the situation, assume the *half smile and willing hands* position: With your elbows at your sides, hold your hands out, palms up, like you're waiting for someone to give you something. Arrange your face into a half smile—not a full smile, but as if you're getting your face "into position" to smile. Turn your lips up ever so slightly to a degree that would most likely not be notice-able to an observer. You'll probably feel awkward or self-conscious the first few times, but that's okay—and it will pass when you realize that it works!

Doing both physical motions together actually helps us physically feel more willing and accepting—it's a willing posture, essentially with the opposite effect of crossing your arms. (If doing them separately or choosing just one feels better or is more effective, go ahead and do that.) Our bodies communicate directly to our minds, even when we're not consciously aware of it; that's where body language comes from.

(Not convinced? Give this exercise a try the next time you find your-self embroiled in a power struggle with your kid.)

Opposite Action

Opposite action is the epitome of "fake it till you make it"—it's being aware of your own emotions and doing the opposite of what your instincts are telling you. This skill is useful for encouraging acceptance during those times when the last thing you want to do is accept, or when you really want to accept but you're just not feeling it.

This isn't stifling or pushing away your feelings. You can feel the emo-tions—just act as if you don't. Ask yourself: *If I were accepting of my child, how would I act right now?* And then go do it.

When your son has pushed his limits to the max and you just want to throttle him, try giving him a kiss instead. When your daughter has called you a bad mommy for the third time and you're really feeling like one, smile instead of crying. When you feel like screaming, whisper.

It's okay if your feelings don't feel genuine while trying opposite action. After all, you're faking it! Your body will send a message of acceptance to your brain, confusing it just enough to put the brakes on an unhelpful emotion. When you fake it, you actually will make it—the faking will lead to a change in your emotions. Remember, though, that your child can sense your authenticity, so be sure to go totally opposite—halfway isn't going to cut it (and it also won't have the full effect on your emotion).

Practice this skill during quiet times—imagining yourself putting it into action, which you'll learn more about next—and it will be easier to implement during challenging times.

Cope Ahead

Feeling overwhelmed by these new skills? Don't be! It takes time to get used to them and to find out which ones work best for you and your child.

This last skill is unique; it offers you an opportunity to practice your other skills. Practicing acceptance strategies in high-stress situations is rarely effective and very difficult, so how else can you rehearse them?

Cope ahead helps you test out and practice other skills without the heat-of-the-moment pressure. This skill is a powerful tool in parenting—and in life in general. You've probably done it in some capacity: thought about exactly how you'd do something better if you had a do-over (like all those times that you've thought of the *perfect* comeback in the shower, hours after the conversation). Guess what? You *do* get a do-over in most parenting situations because chances are good that you'll find yourself in the same position at some point in the future.

Using imagery—picturing yourself in the situation in your mind's eye, as if you are experiencing the moment—is a powerful tool. Research shows that the same areas of the brain that are activated during imagery are also activated during the actual activity (Jeannerod and Frak 1999). That's why athletes and actors use imagery when they prepare for their games or performances; it's proven to improve the real-life execution. That's the principle underlying the cope ahead strategy.

Here's how to cope ahead:

At a calm, quiet time, sit quietly and replay a commonly recurring scene in your mind: your child loses control, you get frustrated and start thinking (or saying) nonaccepting statements, you keep getting stuck in ineffective patterns, you fight the reality of your child's reality…and everyone comes out a loser. (Write out the details if that helps you.)

Then change the script, visualizing and imagining yourself engaging and responding in a more appropriate fashion. Be realistic: include the thoughts and emotions that usually come up in these situations as well as your child's responses (just because you're acting effectively doesn't mean that he will follow suit). Imagine your responses and your emotions, using your preferred acceptance strategies. This will make it easier for you to navigate similar situations in the future.

Strategies to Reach Radical Acceptance

All of the above acceptance strategies can help you move closer to—and eventually achieve—radical acceptance. Other techniques that can ease the path to acceptance include the following:

- **Observe yourself when interacting with your child.** Ask yourself: *Am I observing any rage, frustration, or irritation with myself or my child right now? Am I accepting reality or fighting it?*

- **Look at causes that may have led to the situation.** Examine factors such as life events, temperament (yours or your child's), family dynamics, learning or school-related issues, and parenting skills. It's easier to accept when you can identify what created the situation that's causing you anguish.

- **Let go of blame.** Don't blame yourself, others, or any other factors. Blaming leads to bitterness and resentment, which can get in the way of completely accepting the reality. Realize that everything has a cause; don't excuse or justify that cause, but don't hold onto the blame either.

- **Make meaning.** Turn to religion, prayer, or other meaningful channels of your life. Many find it comforting to believe that there is a greater significance to their pain; try phrases such as *this is what's best for me; this is God's plan, and it's beyond my comprehension; this will help me be a better person.*

- **Embrace change.** (Again, that doesn't mean you have to like it.) The more you think, *I don't want to deal with this; this shouldn't be happening to me,* the more stuck you will get. Change will always be a part of your life; understanding that fact will help you be more flexible and accepting of change.

- **Let your emotions arise.** It's okay to be upset. The five stages of grief first proposed by Elisabeth Kübler-Ross in 1969—denial, anger, bargaining, depression, and last, acceptance—are all normal and to be expected. There's no "right" way to grieve (which is why the five stages are often reorganized by mental health professionals). When someone experiences the death of a loved one, it's painful to start sorting through their belongings, but it's a necessary step on the path to peace. Similarly, you can and should allow yourself to mourn the loss of your ideal reality in order to achieve acceptance.

Acceptance in Action

There are infinite scenarios that arise in parenting—of both the everyday, minor variety and the significant, life-changing variety—that require your acceptance. Depending on the particular situation and on your own personality, you can choose one or several acceptance strategies to help you move toward acceptance.

These scenes may seem familiar to you; read through them to learn how to apply the acceptance skills to various situations that may crop up in your own life.

Situation 1: The Storm After the Calm

You've raised two angelic kids, beloved by everyone—from teachers to coaches to storeowners to grouchy great aunts—and you're (rightfully) proud of your parenting skills. Life's coasting along...until child number three arrives.

And he's a tornado in your little oasis of calm.

This child is unmanageable. He's moody. He's dysregulated. He flies into a rage over everything. Your home is suddenly overtaken by screaming and temper tantrums, by alphabet-soup diagnoses and countless therapy appointments. He's irritable, with a hair-trigger temper, and he's affecting everyone and everything in the house. He has trouble with transitions and authority. In short, he's not like any child you've ever dealt with, and he's wreaked havoc on your family from day one.

You don't want to accept the fact that your third child is the kind of kid you used to shake your head at in carpool line (*Who is raising that child?!*). Instead, you keep trying to fix him. *His sister never talked to me like that! This is totally unacceptable! I can't put up with this! This child is a nutcase and he's ruining our family!*

What did you do wrong? And what can you do right?

Try these acceptance skills as you traverse this new and rocky parenting path:

- **Opposite action:** When you're feeling angry and annoyed at your child's behavior and find yourself overwhelmed by the urge to cry, yell, engage, punish, or worse, collect your strength and do the opposite: laugh, smile, hug, end the conversation, or leave the room.

- **Pros and cons:** Take a break from fighting reality and draw up a pros and cons chart of accepting your child the way he is. (*Sample pros:* I won't be so stressed out all the time; he'll feel better about himself, and his therapist says he's lacking self-esteem. *Sample cons:* he'll think this behavior is okay; I'll have to admit that he's different and that my control is limited; I'm incredibly sad and upset that we will continue living like this and our situation may not change.)

- **Connect to accept:** It's extra-hard to connect to a child who feels foreign to you, but it's even more important to connect with him *because* he's so different. Take some time (preferably on one of his better days) to reflect on his complexities, and you'll probably find that he's not as foreign as you thought.

- **Cope ahead:** Be prepared to deal with the thoughts of nonacceptance and frustration that will inevitably arise. Imagine yourself using your new skills, and practice, practice, practice.

Situation 2: The Personality Disparity

You're the brainiac in the family. The organized one. The athlete. The goody-goody. The social butterfly. The perfectionist. The all-around kid who sailed through school, and then through life…until you give birth to your polar opposite.

This child doesn't resemble you in any way, shape, or form. He daydreams. He talks back. He's an average student at best. His room looks like the "before" pictures from an episode of *Hoarders*. He has a couple of friends and a couple of left feet. He lives in a constant state of irritability, with not-infrequent flare-ups of fury.

Where did this kid come from?

You love him dearly, but it's just so hard to relate to him.

At different stages of life and in various interactions, you can use your acceptance skills:

- **Pros and cons:** You may use this skill in two different ways.

  1. List the pros and cons of accepting your son's personality. You're not going to change him, so one pro might be avoiding the frustration (for both of you) that would surely result from trying to make him be like you. The cons may include having to come to terms with the fact that you can't relate to your child on some levels.

  2. Identify the positives of your son's personality as compared to yours. He may enjoy a slower, less pressured way of life than you do; his scatterbrained tendencies correspond with artistic skill; he is nicer to his siblings than you were to yours because he's not as competitive as you are. (You're naturally familiar with the cons; write them down anyway. Seeing them written out will help you come to terms with them and validate your difficulty in accepting.)

- **Connect to accept:** While working on pros and cons, you'll likely uncover a lot of positive traits in your son. Write them down and review them when you're feeling especially frustrated with him.

- **Look for similarities:** His music preferences are similar to yours. You both scrape the cream off of your Oreos with your teeth before dunking them. You have the same laugh. He wears braces just like you did. You're both passionate about animal rescue. Find any and all similarities!

- **Cope ahead:** You'll inevitably face many, many situations in which you'll wish your child were different, and you'll experience that disappointment and frustration again and again. Picture yourself focusing on his teacher's praise at parent-teacher conferences (instead of on his dismal grades); rehearse your response to your mother the next time she asks *again* why he doesn't play soccer like you did; practice breathing deeply and speaking calmly to him the next time you tackle room cleaning. Remind yourself that this is exactly as he *should* be.

Situation 3: The Divergent Life Choices

For years, you dreamed about walking your child into her Ivy League dorm; you dreamed of giving her everything you weren't able to have. You padded her college fund accordingly, signed her up for AP classes and enrichment courses, and helped her with her homework and extracurriculars to spruce up her GPA and her resume.

But then she threw you for a loop by deciding to go to fashion school instead.

You should've seen the signs; she's always been into fashion (and, frankly, she's good at it). As your visions of watching her graduate dissipate before your eyes, you can use various skills to cope with your disappointment and accept her choices.

- **Turn your mind:** There will be many milestones (and lack thereof) on your daughter's journey that will remind you, often painfully, of your unfulfilled dream. Every time something comes up—your friend's child's Ivy League graduation, your daughter's first major project and first major rejection—consciously turn your mind toward acceptance, as many times as it takes. Find a comforting thought to turn to at those times: *She's using her talents. She is doing what she loves. She is forging her own path.*

- **Cope ahead:** Most of the disappointing or upsetting moments—like graduation—come with a warning. Imagine yourself encouraging and congratulating your daughter on her milestone and her accomplishments (and do it genuinely, even if you don't feel it…remember the power of opposite action!).

- **Pros and cons:** You may use this skill in two different ways.

  1. List the pros and cons of accepting your daughter's choice versus fighting it: a supportive and understanding relationship versus a strained one, the ability to look toward the future rather than at what could have been.

  2. List the pros and cons of fashion school versus Ivy League: fewer years in school, lower tuition, her ability to use her talents, closer proximity. (Chances are you've rehashed the cons plenty of times, but list them anyway; they can help you validate your concerns and lay out all of the facts.)

Situation 4: The Annoying Phase

Your two-year-old has learned to climb out of his crib. Your four-year-old is deep in the "why" phase. Your nine-year-old complains that his siblings always get the better end of the deal and everything is "just not fair." Your tween has morphed into a moody hermit. Your teen rolls her eyes so frequently you've forgotten what color they are.

You know that it's a phase, and that it will pass…but it isn't passing quickly enough.

Several acceptance skills can help you weather the storm with your sanity intact:

- **Opposite action:** When the temptation to give in to your frustration hits, consciously do the opposite of your instinctive response. Resist the urge to answer "Why isn't the sky green?" with "Why do you ask so many questions?" Instead, take a deep breath and reply with a funny answer ("because then we wouldn't be able to see the leaves") or offer to look up the answer, even though it's the last thing you want to do. When you feel like telling your teen to snap out of her mood, offer her a hug and a cookie instead.

- **Willingness versus willfulness:** Toddler's out of the crib again? Notice the way your shoulders are tensing up and your face could be the picture next to "frustration" in the dictionary. Take a moment to assume a half smile and willing hands position—you'll feel calmer as you put him back in for round two (or, more realistically, round seventeen) of bedtime.

- **Embrace change:** Remember your surly stage as a teen? (If you don't, your mom will be thrilled to remind you.) Thinking about your own phases can help you empathize and accept your teen's current angst. Better yet, pull up videos of her in her last phase and remember how you felt then; it will put the current phase into perspective and remind you that there's an end in sight. Remember, change is constant.

- **Connect to accept:** Look beyond the obnoxious behavior, all-consuming as it may seem. List your child's positive traits and ask yourself questions to reconnect with him…preferably when he's sleeping or being particularly cooperative.

Situation 5: The Unforeseen Special Need

Your child has been diagnosed with a learning disability, a health condition, or a neurological disorder. Your life—and hers—has changed and will

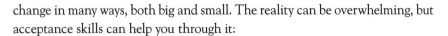

change in many ways, both big and small. The reality can be overwhelming, but acceptance skills can help you through it:

- **Radical acceptance:** You're facing a new reality, and you won't be getting your old reality back. Allow yourself to grieve the loss of that reality and experience the emotions that accompany that loss. You can wish it were different, but don't get stuck; embrace the present. Move toward complete acceptance, letting go of blame, of "should," of willfulness.

- **Turn your mind:** Even absolute acceptance needs a refresher periodically. It's normal to experience disappointment, sadness, and other emotions as your child encounters hurdles or misses milestones, deviating from the life that you envisioned. Find the mantra or method that helps you and turn to that during difficult times.

- **Opposite action:** You *want* to wallow in the despair and fight the unfairness of it all. For your child—and for yourself—go opposite that desire and do what needs to be done, even though it's hard. Those actions may include researching therapy and treatment; scheduling appointments for your child (and yourself); requesting some time off from work; and talking to your child's teacher, principal, or educational coordinator to best address her needs, even while your brain is protesting against it (*This child is fine and doesn't need all this extra help!*).

- **Make meaning:** Many find solace in helping others who are suffering. Try to find the meaning in your new reality: form or join a support group, raise money for research, or simply tell yourself that this is what *should* be happening in your life (a thought that you may find very freeing). Accept that this is part of a Master Plan and that everything and everyone has a purpose, even if you can't see it or don't understand it.

Congratulations! You're now armed with a whole new arsenal of practical acceptance strategies and (hopefully) the confidence to use them. Remember, it will take time, patience, practice, and trial and error to find what works best for you. Be kind to yourself; acceptance is not easy, but the rewards are incomparable. You are a great parent for working on it! Next we'll turn to the practice of mindfulness.

CHAPTER 4

Mindfulness: Lighting the Way

Mindfulness seems to be the buzzword of the day across various age groups, cultures, and industries, but it's not just a "buzz"—it's the fundamental core of DBT and of the concepts defined in this book. It's one of the cornerstones of effective parenting as it helps parents center themselves, understand their children's behavior, clearly define their children's strengths and challenges, and utilize the skills in their arsenals. Mindful parents experience an increase in awareness of when, where, and how to make change.

In this chapter, you'll learn:

- The definition of mindfulness

- Why mindfulness is considered an acceptance skill

- The benefits of mindful parenting

- Mindfulness skills

- Guidelines and mantras to help you implement mindfulness

- How to overcome obstacles to mindfulness

What Is Mindfulness?

Mindfulness is a state of mind, characterized by intentionally living with awareness, openness, and curiosity. When you are mindful, you consciously focus your mind on the present, taking control of your mind rather than allowing your mind to control you; it allows you to let go of judgment and disentangle yourself from the moment so that you can move forward effectively.

Living in the moment, mindfully, helps you get completely in touch with your current reality.

Think of mindfulness as a lamp. You can enter a dark room and choose to grope around in the darkness (and inevitably step on a LEGO), or you can flip on the lamp and find what you're looking for immediately. Mindfulness shines a light on the nooks and crannies of your life, helping you focus and increasing your effectiveness.

Our minds can be chaotic; mindfulness helps us harness, quiet, and center our minds to focus on what's important. It's a critical skill for parents, whose minds are often more "full" than those of nonparents!

Are you *mind-full*—with your mind overloaded with schedules/appointments/friendships/schoolwork/concerning behaviors/extracurricular activities/safety/college fund…and the list goes on (no wonder you're so frazzled!)—or *mindful*?

Mind-Full or Mindful?

Why Is Mindfulness an Acceptance Strategy?

Mindfulness is crucial for both acceptance and change, and it helps us focus on each situation individually to decide whether acceptance or change—or both—is in order. Picture a grilled cheese sandwich. When you first assemble it, you have bread and cheese that just happen to be placed next to each other; add it to a hot frying pan and you get a delicious meal. Mindfulness is that heat that melds acceptance and change into one entity, transforming two separate items into one.

Like all acceptance strategies, mindfulness can lead to change; however, mindfulness is a unique subset of acceptance. It's a state of being rather than an active "doing" technique. Other acceptance skills are designed to achieve acceptance, while the goal of mindfulness is simply to be present. That state of being present is the essence of acceptance: living in the moment without doing anything to change it, being completely open and curious about the moment at hand, and allowing whatever is happening to happen.

The goal of acceptance is to *become*—become connected to the reality and the facts of your life. The goal of mindfulness, on the other hand, is to *be*.

Even when mindfulness doesn't help you know what to do next, it helps you get into the right frame of mind to balance acceptance and change. It's pure acceptance without any change at all (though change is often a bonus result!).

The Benefits of Mindful Parenting

Now, before you flip right past this section (*I am so not the yoga/meditation type; mindfulness is too New Age for me*), here's why mindfulness is an important goal.

Mindfulness provides multiple benefits in different areas of your life. It benefits you, your child (and other members of the family), and your parent-child relationship.

When you're mindful, you experience every moment as is, both internally and externally. This allows you to be present and composed during parent-hood's most challenging (and most rewarding) moments. You'll feel the effects of mindfulness physically (calmer nerves and lower heart rates), emotionally (improved emotional regulation and a quieter, peaceful mind), and mentally (improved focus and decision-making abilities).

Mindfulness also benefits your child. When practiced effectively, mindfulness helps you understand and accept your child's behaviors as they are, without getting stuck in your analyses, interpretations, and judgments.

In addition to the individual advantages of mindfulness, it promotes a healthy connection between you and your child. The positive interactions created through mindfulness help your child sense your love and affection, which builds a healthy parent-child attachment and boosts your child's self-confidence. Mindful parenting is designed to lead to a heightened understanding of your child, which directly affects your feelings toward him and enhances the relationship.

You know in your very bones that your child is at the forefront of your mind. Being present with her helps her know it and feel it, too. Think about it: when you consciously allow yourself to fully experience the joyful moments of parenting—no matter how small—you form a priceless, unbreakable bond with your child. When you take your child to the park, you may be tempted to catch up on emails or just enjoy a few minutes to yourself, but if you take the time and effort to be present with him, you create an irreplaceable shared experience.

Of course, as an acceptance strategy, mindfulness also helps us change. It grants us the awareness that's so necessary in defining our specific challenges and goals to move toward change. It sheds light on our own thoughts, emotions, behaviors, and reactions, which helps us respond effectively.

Skeptical? Try it and see for yourself. Mindfulness is within reach with specific skills and practices. Of course, like any skill, it takes time and practice, so be patient!

Achieving Mindfulness

Mindfulness is an active, ongoing process; it's not a state of mind that you achieve once and retain forever. Don't worry about "messing up"—when you slip up, let your thoughts drift, make a snap judgment, or get stuck, that's all part of the process. The very act of catching yourself and bringing yourself back to the proper state of mind is actually mindfulness!

If you're thinking that you are too busy for this, rest assured that mindfulness does not require long meditation-style sessions. In fact, you can incorporate mindfulness into your everyday activities and interactions.

There are six main mindfulness skills that will help you along your journey to mindfulness. These strategies will allow you to clearly define the challenges that you need to address in order to parent effectively. Linehan (2015) grouped the skills into two categories: "what" skills and "how" skills.

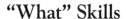

"What" Skills

The first set of skills focuses on *what* you can do to work toward mindfulness. These skills can only be practiced and implemented one at a time; each one can help you achieve a mindful, present state of mind, and different situations call for the use of different skills.

"What" Skill #1: Observe

Observing is a passive skill rather than an active one (but that doesn't mean that it doesn't require significant mental energy!): it's quietly paying attention to the present moment and the present moment only.

Pick any moment and simply observe what's going on around you—events, emotions, and behaviors, both inside and outside yourself. Use all of your five senses to observe your surroundings and your internal senses to observe your own physical and mental responses.

Sounds easy? Give it a try! You may be surprised by how wired you are to get caught up in your thoughts, analyze the situation, and actively think. When you observe your thoughts, you don't put effort into thinking; you simply allow the thoughts to happen and notice them as they do.

The act of observing is controlling your attention, not your reactions or surroundings. It's like sitting on the platform at a train station and idly watching the trains go by; this skill is all about observing your trains of thought and watching where they go. Even if you find yourself on one of those trains, racing down the track, you can jump back off and return to your observation post.

Why Observe?

Every parent can benefit from observing. Do you frequently find yourself caught in spiraling situations—you know the ones, when you find yourself wondering just what happened after it's all over—or stuck in an emotional state without quite knowing how you got there? Observing opens your mind to the moment at hand. It holds the key to revealing the causes of emotions and behaviors (both positive and negative).

Observing "flips on the light" in your darkened room. It's the most basic step to bring the present into focus so that you can gather the facts with curiosity and an open mind. Observers learn valuable information by watching; when you observe, you'll gather information about yourself, your children, and your parenting—pieces of information that you'd likely miss if you were analyzing the situation further.

Observing may help you notice your own judgmental thoughts or assumptions; you'll start to identify thoughts as thoughts, not as facts. Taking a step back and observing gives you a bit of distance and detachment from your own thoughts and emotions so that you can recognize and regulate them. This will help you get "unstuck" from unhelpful emotions, controlling those emotions rather than allowing them to control you.

The act of observing can be a challenge at first. Your mind is used to wandering off where it pleases! Think of it as training your brain and gently, repeatedly redirect your thoughts to the present.

Ever trained a puppy? Your mind is like that overeager puppy, running around gleefully despite your attempts at obedience training. At first, you loosen the leash, giving the puppy space to run while gently reining him in; with time, patience, and consistent redirection, he'll eventually learn to respond to your commands…and so will your mind.

A typical parenting moment may look like this without mindfulness:

Scene: Kids playing in the backyard

Mom's thoughts: *Look at that. Jessica's doing so well on the monkey bars! I've got to remember to tell her gymnastics coach. But Jake can't seem to climb that ladder. Maybe he needs occupational therapy. I wonder if the kids make fun of him because he's so uncoordinated. I'll make a note to call the teacher. He looks like he's getting frustrated.*

Oh, great. Now she's teasing him. Why can't she ever be nice to her brother? He's totally going to hit her and then I'll have two crying kids. This is a disaster! Better get involved before this spirals completely out of control. There goes our nice afternoon…again.

Mom—as parents naturally do—may think she's observing, but in actuality, she's thinking, evaluating, judging, reflecting. She's reading into everything and her thoughts are (understandably) all over the place, making her anxious and causing her to act impulsively.

What would the situation look like with mindfulness?

When Mom practices mindful observing, the narrative in her mind stops. (Yes, that constant running commentary *can* be quieted.) She'll sit on her lounge chair and observe the little details—Jake's facial expression, Jessica's posture, her own spike in blood pressure—that she may have missed while caught in her thoughts.

These observations will help her generate a fuller picture of what's going on—perhaps Jake stuck his tongue out at Jessica before she started teasing him; maybe Mom will notice that her own shoulders tense up before she gets angry at the kids. She'll notice thoughts as thoughts, emotions as emotions, bodily responses as bodily responses, judgments as interpretations. She'll observe the anxiety that she feels and the thoughts that she thinks without acting on them. These observations will allow her to understand her children, connect with them, and meet their needs effectively.

AN OBSERVE EXERCISE

Watch your kids as they engage in a typical activity—playing a game, taking a bath, doing homework—and observe the thoughts that flow in and out of your mind without attempting to control them. Stay present as you observe them without acting on any thoughts, emotions, or impulses. Keep yourself grounded by consciously focusing on and observing your breath as you naturally inhale and exhale.

"What" Skill #2: Describe

Describing builds on observing and is a more active skill. It's putting your observations—and your observations only—into words.

Why Describe?

If you frequently find yourself assigning explanations and making assumptions based on your observations, describing the facts at hand can help you remove yourself from the situation—especially an emotionally charged one—and recognize what's happening.

Describing helps you put your observations into concrete, factual, nonjudgmental words.

This can be especially useful when you describe your emotions. Putting a name to your emotion accomplishes two things: (1) it helps you make sense of that emotion and validate it, which leads to self-regulation and self-control, and (2) it helps you realize that you are not your emotion, which allows you to distance yourself from the emotion and decide whether or not to act on that emotion.

Additionally, the Describe skill facilitates clear communication with benefits for you and your child:

- **For you:** Describing helps you differentiate between facts and emotions, between thoughts and incidents, and between events and responses to those events by labeling each separately. Contrast your mindful description (*He dropped the glass; the glass shattered; I noticed that my heart rate jumped*) with your unmindful description (*He's so irresponsible; he destroyed another glass; this child has no regard for our possessions; why does he insist on making my life miserable?*).

- **For your child:** Getting all the facts out on the table sets the foundation for effective, blameless, nonthreatening communication that gets everyone on the same page before attempting to find a solution.

The Describe skill can be useful both in your own head and in communication with others. You can describe the situations, emotions, and behaviors that you observe to yourself, silently, to help you identify the components of the interaction. You can also use this skill out loud, in communication, to factually describe the different facets of the situation at hand. This will help get everyone's cards laid out on the table before attempting to problem solve.

Whether you're describing to yourself or to others, the "rules" are the same.

The trick is to describe *only* what you've observed. That means that anything you can't observe doesn't count. Nonobservable facts include other people's thoughts, emotions, or intentions ("He did that just to make me crazy!") and events that haven't happened yet, even if you "know" that it's inevitable ("I can see from the look on her face that we're in for a fight").

Use descriptive words to recount what happened or what you felt or saw. Don't interpret! Say (or think), "She rolled her eyes at me" rather than "She has a bad attitude this morning." If you remove the judgment from your description, you may be surprised to learn that your child had an eyelash in her eye (and if you'd launched right into "Don't roll your eyes at me," it likely would have exploded into an actual bad attitude). When you describe the facts objectively, you give your child an opportunity to correct you. And when the facts are laid out, you may discover that your thoughts were colored by judgment and interpretation!

Similarly, describe your thoughts and feelings as just that—thoughts and feelings, not facts— which helps you gain some of that aforementioned distance from them. (Remember: describing helps you differentiate between feelings and facts.)

Try it! Say (or think): "I'm feeling angry" rather than "I am angry"—that single word, "feeling," places distance between you and your anger. Similarly, replace "I'm a bad parent" with "I had the thought that I'm a bad parent"—that differentiates between fact and thoughts.

Remember Jessica and Jake, who were playing on the monkey bars? If their mom mindfully described the backyard scene (out loud, to herself, or in writing), it would sound something like this:

Jessica is swinging all the way across the monkey bars. I'm thinking that I should tell her gymnastics coach how well she's doing. She's smiling and her eyes are sparkling!

Jake keeps slipping off the ladder. His legs don't stretch far enough. He's getting red in the face. Jessica is calling him a baby. His eyes are starting to tear and he's walking in her direction. I notice that I'm starting to feel annoyed and upset at Jessica.

Rather than ascribing labels to the scene in front of her (*She looks so pleased with herself* or *He's getting angry now* or *She's being mean to him*), Mom now has an unbiased description of what's happening. Those descriptions will help her identify and articulate different factors so that she can be calmly effective.

Realistically, you will not be able to describe everything all the time, nor should you expect to. Try practicing the skill a few times a day in nonconfrontational settings, even one small description at a time. At first, you'll probably need to do it deliberately. The more you practice, the easier and more natural it will become for you to see the facts and to describe mindfully, without analyzing or jumping to conclusions.

A DESCRIBE EXERCISE

Examine a picture (or, better yet, a video) of your child. Describe his expression and as many details as you can without naming emotions (say, "His eyebrows are drawn and his mouth is turned down" rather than "He looks sad"). Notice that describing the facts (and only the facts) helps you avoid interpretations and judgment, letting you see your child for exactly who and what he is.

"What" Skill #3: Participate

There's a time and place for everything, and while less active skills such as Observe and Describe should be used at some times and in some places, there are times to actively Participate.

Participating is the act of being present and engaged in the moment rather than being a passive bystander. It's throwing yourself completely into the present without self-consciousness or thoughts like *What is everyone else thinking?* True participation is the goal of mindfulness.

The other "what" skills (Observe and Describe) are tools that help you achieve the Participate skill.

The next time the Olympics air, pay close attention to the participants' faces. If their attention wavers, their performance falters; they perform at their top level only when they're completely present in the moment. Olympians win medals by *fully* participating in their competition.

The same goes for parenting. In order to be an effective parent, you'll need to fully participate in the experience, the emotions, and the moments. And while you may throw yourself into some of the more exciting bits of parenting—her big game, his graduation, their pillow fight—you also need to allow yourself to experience the everyday moments of discipline, negative emotion, and monotony.

When something goes wrong, the Olympian's coach (who has been observing all along) is tasked with describing the issue in order to improve the athlete's performance.

Likewise, when your participation isn't working for you or your child, it's time to take a step back and return to observing and describing. Think of it like crossing the street: first you stop, look, and listen (Observe and Describe), and then you cross when it's safe (Participate).

Why Participate?

The ultimate goal of parenting is attentive participation (though some moments call for less active involvement). As much as you don't want to admit it, your empty-nesting neighbor was right—these parenting moments are fleeting (though they seem endless now).

Feeling awkward? That's normal, but don't allow it to stop you. You may feel inclined to sit on a towel under your beach umbrella and watch your children build a sand castle, just like your parents did when you were a kid (*Hey, I turned out okay, didn't I?*). When you participate in that moment—go over and show them some of your best building tips, help them gather buckets full of damp sand, dig the moat, let them bury you without thinking about *how on earth you're going to get all that sand out of your hair*—you're creating a special connection and a shared experience between yourself and your child.

Participation encourages you to be fully present in your own life and the lives of your children. When you're involved in their moments—even the smallest moments—you experience parenthood at a more profound level than you would as an observer. It also allows you to recognize the fleeting nature of every moment, which increases flexibility as you roll with the constant ebb and flow of life.

To fully participate, let go of thoughts about how you look to others (even to your own kids) as you maneuver yourself into the ball pit. Forget about the laundry you'll have to do after the mud-pie baking contest. Dismiss your recollection of yesterday's less-than-enthusiastic reaction to the rule you instituted. Allow yourself to experience the here and now (of course, without recklessness, thoughtlessness, or irresponsibility—you're still the grownup!).

Participation isn't just for the joyful moments in parenting. When you participate fully in disciplining your child, it shows him that you're serious about it, rather than casually throwing out directions and admonishments.

Remember Jessica and Jake's mom? Now that her internal dialogue has ended, she's helping Jake get his little legs up on the ladder, cheering with Jessica as she jumps off the monkey bars, and chiding Jessica for teasing her brother.

A PARTICIPATE EXERCISE

Allow yourself to experience a moment in your day—a conversation, an event, a meal—as a full participant, without focusing on other distractions or planning the next item on your schedule.

Sing a silly song to your child—or, on the flipside, discipline her—without wondering who's listening and how they're judging you, without second-guessing or guilting yourself.

"How" Skills

Now that you know *what* to do, it's time to learn *how* to do it. The second set of skills focuses on *how* to be mindful: nonjudgmentally, "one-mindfully," and effectively. These skills can be used individually or all at once (for best results).

"How" Skill #1: Nonjudgmentally

Nobody likes to be judged. As an adult, you tend to avoid the judgy-mommy neighbor, the teacher who not so subtly disapproves of your parenting style, the mother-in-law whose judgment you can *just see in her eyes* every time she watches you discipline her grandchild. So then why, as a parent, do you judge your child (and yourself, for that matter)?

Don't get defensive; since your child's infancy, you've intuitively judged her. You knew which newborn cry meant she was hungry or scared or tired; you knew exactly which expression heralded an oncoming toddler eruption; you knew that an unexpected change in schedule would mean a full-fledged meltdown. Those judgments are important and useful; the trouble begins when you veer into labeling (good/bad) and your judgment becomes unhelpful and harmful.

It's perfectly natural for you to judge your child, and that's why it can be challenging to Observe, Describe, and Participate in a Nonjudgmental manner.

When you practice mindfulness without judgment, you notice and acknowledge the facts without evaluating them. Your judgments are likely automatic: hitting is bad, cleaning up is good, back talk is terrible, listening right away is expected. Being nonjudgmental takes those labels and assessments completely out of the equation and focuses solely on the facts.

Now, that does *not* mean that you should look at the bright side of every behavior ("Oh look, he's arguing again, he'll make such a great lawyer one day if I manage to survive his childhood!"). Keep reading to learn why and how to suspend that judgment entirely.

Why be nonjudgmental?

Judgment is an obstacle to effective behavior for several reasons:

1. **It gets in the way of change.** Judgment rarely leads to an effective solution. It prevents you from dealing with the situation logically and objectively: your preconceived notions and feelings can cloud your vision and skew your viewpoint, adding complicating factors to even the simplest interactions. Plus—even with your child, whose every expression, every mood change, every nuance is so familiar to you—judgments are not always accurate, thanks to that clouded vision.

2. **It leads to negative emotion.** In addition to clouding your vision when it comes to the facts, judgment triggers the emotional part of your mind. That trigger leads to negative emotions and unhelpful behavior.

3. **It hurts relationships.** Children are sensitive, intuitive creatures, just like adults. They'll pick up on your judgment, which can cause poor self-esteem (*I'm bad; even my mom thinks so*) and lead them to believe that it's not worth trying to meet your expectations (*Why should I work*

so hard when my efforts aren't even appreciated?). This pattern of think-ing—self-criticism and unrelenting standards for themselves—may follow them into adulthood.

Don't forget about self-judgment. As human beings, we tend to be our own harshest critics. When you judge your own parenting (*I'm a failure as a mother; I can't even get my kids to listen to me*), you lessen your ability to parent effectively.

Hey, you're reading this book; that says a lot about you as a parent. Give yourself a pat on the back! Sitting around and judging yourself will accomplish nothing except for making you feel bad. Instead, observe the facts to figure out where change would be most helpful.

We'll take a brief detour here to discuss an important point: the pitfalls of "should."

Anyone who has used the word "should" (myself included) is guilty of being judgmental. Parents constantly tell me about their children's shortcom-ings: "She shouldn't be lying to me!" "He should know better than to hit his brother!" "They shouldn't come home past curfew!" "She should not be failing chemistry!"

My answer always catches them off guard: "Yes, your child *should* be [hitting/lying/flunking/[insert offense here]." She *should* be doing it—because she *is* doing it! When you project your opinions and judgments onto your child's behavior, you get caught up in what she "should" be doing—while forgetting to focus on what she *is* doing.

Your child *should* be engaging in that behavior, because that behavior has a cause. You (and your child) may not know what that cause is, but *everything is as it should be* under the circumstances.

If you concentrate on what "should" be, you miss an important part of the equation: the underlying cause and the situation that's actually at hand. Judgment will obscure your view of the big picture and hinder effective change. Once you get past the tunnel vision of judgment and get a good look at the behavior and its causes, you'll be able to work on problem solving.

Furthermore, when your child doesn't meet your expectations (because they're unrealistic for him in his current state), you will start to feel frustrated with him. That frustration—even if you don't verbalize it—will cause your child to feel unaccepted, which will lead him to feel unmotivated to change... and he'll continue to fall short of your expectations.

Of course, as a responsible parent, you'd prefer that he didn't engage in these behaviors. You *do* want him to know how he "should" behave. Don't completely strike the word "should" from your vocabulary. Use "should" in a positive manner when explaining appropriate and expected behaviors, values, and morals to your child: "You should be kind to others." "You should ask your sister nicely next time." "You should come tell us if somebody hurts you."

So what is the key to being nonjudgmental? It starts with paying attention.

Pay attention to your thoughts; you'll notice yourself automatically ascribing judgment (both positive and negative) to virtually everything around you. (Pay attention to your emotions, too—frustration and agitation often accompany judgment, so you may notice that before you actually notice the judging.) Catch yourself (without judging yourself!) and work on acknowledging facts as facts, without good/bad (or even neutral) labels.

Now, being nonjudgmental doesn't mean that you are ignoring problems. It's quite the opposite. You are recognizing problem behavior (and its ramifications) without labeling it as good or bad.

Imagine your child has a tend0y to lie. You can describe the situation in two ways:

- **Judgmentally:** *This kid is such a liar! I can't believe a word that comes out of his mouth. The school keeps harping on it like I can control him somehow. This behavior is horrible; it's making my life a living nightmare!*

- **Nonjudgmentally:** *When my child lies, I feel frustrated. His teacher is having difficulty dealing with and tolerating his behavior. We need to find a solution for the lying and acting out.*

You're not trying to find the positive in every situation (*He comes up with the most creative lies!*); instead, you're matter-of-factly focusing on the behavior and its outcomes in order to address it properly. Sure, finding the positive in your child is a wonderful skill and you should definitely employ it. However, even positive judgment is judgment, so try to drop all judgment while practicing being nonjudgmental. Once it comes more naturally to you, you can judge positively again.

A NONJUDGMENTAL EXERCISE

Describe your child. There's just one catch: you're only allowed to use observable descriptions (physical characteristics and other tangible facts). That means no judgmental language: no *he's bossy, she's headstrong, he's obedient, she's eager to please.* You can replace those judgmental statements with *He usually responds quickly when I ask him to do something* or *She frequently offers to help around the house—she seems eager to please me.*

Notice your emotional state? It's probably a bit detached, and that's exactly how you want it to be.

Now try it with someone you dislike. (Judgy Mommy or mother-in-law, here's looking at you!) Remember: only observable descriptions. *She is tall and blonde. She plays games with my daughter. She gives me advice. We carpool to soccer. When my mother-in-law watches me take care of my kids, I notice that I start thinking that she disapproves of my parenting, and that makes me feel hurt and frustrated.*

Did you notice a milder emotional response (less annoyance, less aversion, less tension) when you avoided judgment? That's the magic of being nonjudgmental: it takes the emotion out of the encounter so that you can focus on the facts. And focusing on the facts helps you keep your emotions in check and effectively improve your relationships.

It's okay to notice a judgmental thought (*I had the thought that she thinks she's better than me*)—as a matter of fact, it's a great starting point for Nonjudgmental practice. Notice those judgmental thoughts and label them, as we learned with the Describe skill. When you take note of a thought and identify it as judgmental, you essentially deal with it on some level—even if you haven't actually done anything—which makes it easier for you to let it go.

"How" Skill #2: One-Mindfully

This one's a biggie in today's tech-driven world, a world that's faster paced and more accessible—yet simultaneously more demanding and less personal—than ever before.

Acting one-mindfully is the opposite of multitasking. It's staying focused on the task or moment at hand, slowing down your pace, and doing one thing at a time (imagine that!). When you concentrate on doing something one-mindfully, you devote all of your attention to that something (or a segment of a more complex "something")—no distractions, no wandering thoughts, no interruptions.

Why be one-mindful?

As a parent who's tasked with keeping countless balls in the air, performing tasks one-mindfully may seem counterproductive (if not impossible). However, as you begin to apply the skill to your everyday tasks and interactions, you'll realize that replacing multitasking with one-mindfulness actually helps you be *more* productive, effective, and present.

Don't take my word for it—a recent study (Mittelstädt and Miller 2017) showed that multitasking is less efficient. It takes your brain extra time and energy to shift gears as you divide your attention between more than one task. You'd get each task done faster and more effectively if you devoted that extra brainpower to the entire task.

Staying focused on one thing at a time allows you to be present in your life and to avoid getting sidetracked by the million little (and not-so-little) distractions that constantly crop up. This is especially true in parenting, where conversations and interactions tend to veer off course on a regular basis. Plus, in a challenging situation, getting caught up in thoughts of the past and the future can get in the way of being present in the moment and make you feel more overwhelmed, upset, frustrated, or otherwise emotional.

There's a reason why texting while driving is illegal: your brain is not wired to focus optimally on two tasks at once. When you divide your attention among tasks, those tasks take longer to complete and are less likely to be done adequately. Multitasking may be valued in today's society (*after all, why accomplish just one thing when you can accomplish three in the same amount of time?*) but being one-mindful is far more valuable—and surprisingly more efficient.

Now, that doesn't mean that you have to spend untold amounts of time focusing on small tasks. Being one-mindful and accomplishing your to-do list aren't mutually exclusive. Go ahead and work through those complex, multistep tasks or switch from one task to the next quickly—just be sure to focus completely on each task (or step) during that moment, even if the moment lasts for mere seconds.

Additionally, being one-mindful is extremely beneficial for your children. When you make time to be completely present with your child, you're sending her a powerful message: *You are important. You are loved. You are accepted.*

Your child naturally craves your undivided attention and affection. When you are distracted—by household chores awaiting your attention, by a phone call, by another child, by your email—you send a subtle yet clear message to your child: *There is something more important than you.*

You don't intend to send that message, and you certainly don't believe it yourself, but that's what your child absorbs. While you cannot reasonably focus entirely on your child for her entire waking hours, you can carve out valuable quality time in which you focus exclusively on her.

How can you be one-mindful?

Give the matter at hand—the sinkful of dishes, your favorite TV show, your kids' argument, the conversation about your day—your full, undivided attention. When your mind wanders (as it inevitably will, especially in the beginning), gently but firmly bring it back to whatever it is you're supposed to be paying attention to (yes, even the bubbles in the sink or the warmth of the laundry waiting to be folded).

Repeat: *just this one moment, just this one step, just this one breath.* Remember that every moment is brief and precious, and treat it accordingly. When you stop and pay attention to the moment, you'll realize how much you miss out on when you don't focus completely on what's in front of you. Focus on the now; let go of thoughts of the past or future that get in the way of experiencing the present.

Again, the more you practice, the better "training" your brain gets. A personal example: my phone once broke for a few days, leaving me feeling uneasy and adrift, but at the same time (dialectics!) I realized that I was more present without the constant presence (and distraction) of my phone. We don't even realize how often we glance at the phone, how we're distracted by the vibrating even if we don't answer (*Who could that be? Could it be important? Should I just check quickly?*). Since then, I've started putting my phone away in a drawer for short periods of time, and it's been life altering!

A "ONE-MINDFULLY" EXERCISE

Share a moment with your child: at the park, in the grocery store, at the big game. Quash the desire to chat with a friend or check your emails during the less exciting bits and focus on his reactions, his mannerisms, his expressions. Don't miss the baby's first gummy grin, the emerging reader's adorable mispronunciation of "quinoa," or the sport fan's excitement at the winning home run!

The most precious moments can be the smallest of moments. When you're having a conversation with your child, no matter how mundane (you know, like the one where she's talking about what every single child ate for lunch and snack today), give it your full attention. Put down the phone and let go of the to-do list that's looming ever larger on the fridge. Look her in the eye. Really listen to who had pudding and who traded a bologna sandwich for a PB&J.

When you're one-mindful, it lends importance and weight to the moment—and it's way more effective than the impatient *That's nice, now tell me about your spelling test* that makes your child feel unheard.

No, one-mindfulness doesn't magically create extra hours in the day. However, being one-mindful truly has the power to get that task or conversation completed so that you can move on. Don't believe it? Try it for yourself—at bedtime, homework time, soccer practice time, crunch time, whatever time you believe you *must* multitask—and see the results.

A BONUS "ONE-MINDFULLY" EXERCISE FOR YOU

Try to set a regular "mindful date" with each of your children—especially the challenging one(s)—once a week for ten to twenty minutes. Turn off your phone, announce to the rest of the family that you're busy now and shouldn't be disturbed, and simply spend time in your child's company. Listen to her; play a game with her; sit together quietly...whatever works for that particular child. These little sessions can have a huge impact, filling your child's need for attention in a positive manner (even if she professes to be "too cool" for one-on-one Mom/Dad time.)

"How" Skill #3: Effectively

Finally—and perhaps most importantly—in order to be successful and make progress, your mindful parenting must be effective.

Acting effectively is focusing on *doing what works*. It's recognizing what needs to be done (whether that's seeking a solution or simply listening to your child), both in the moment and in the long term. Effectiveness is the opposite of "cutting off your nose to spite your face"—it's abandoning your notions of "right" or "fair" and concentrating on the end result.

As a therapist, one of my favorite words is "effective." Everyone wants to know if their actions and feelings are "right" or "wrong" or if they're behaving the way they're "supposed to be" behaving. My answer is always the same: don't ask if it's right or wrong, good or bad—ask if it's effective. If you can achieve your goals by doing something the "wrong" way, then by all means, go ahead and do it!

(Of course, there is still a concept of right and wrong on a moral and inter-personal level. You may feel better if you slug an annoying coworker in the face, and it effectively gets him to stop hounding you, but it's still wrong!)

Effectiveness is the key to success. If there were one solution that worked for every parent and child, your child would have come with an owner's manual! Whenever you use a parenting technique from this book or anywhere else, evaluate the effectiveness of it. If it doesn't work, it's time for a change.

Why act effectively?

Many common refrains of parenting are anti-effective: *I've told him 100 times and he still does it! It's simply not right that she acts that way! I will continue to punish him this way until he gets it!*

If you've told your kid something 100 times and he still doesn't listen (though, in a perfect world, he "should"), what makes you think that the 101st time will be the magic time? If you followed the foolproof parenting solution that everyone swears by and it *just didn't work*, does it make sense to continue trying because it works for everyone else?

You can carry out every skill to the letter—you can Observe, Describe, and Participate in a nonjudgmental and one-mindful manner—but if it doesn't help you achieve your goal, what's the point?

Effectiveness values outcome over principle. Sure, when you're stuck behind a driver who's going below the speed limit in the left lane, you can legiti-mately get frustrated: *He should not be driving so slowly! Doesn't he know that this is the fast lane? This is just not right.* You can flash your brights, honk at him, or call the police to report a slow driver. You'd be absolutely right—but you'll also come away upset and annoyed (and it'll probably take you longer to get to your destination!).

What happens if you focus on the end goal instead of getting sidetracked by the Sunday driver in front of you? If you pass the driver and continue on your merry way, you'll get to your destination faster, safer, and calmer. Can't pass? Just focus on your ultimate goal, getting there, and congratulate yourself on your admirable patience. (Remember, road rage endangers lives and causes accidents.)

So you can continue to tell your child, *for the millionth time*, that she needs to put away her shoes. The shoes may get put away, but you'll be frustrated, she'll be frustrated, and she'll leave them out again tomorrow. Or you can choose to be effective and find a solution that will bypass that nagging and the resulting frustration. It may take more time and patience to work on that solu-tion, but you'll achieve both your short-term goal (a neat house) and your ulti-mate goal (daughter putting away her shoes without being nagged every day).

There's a third option: you may choose to decide that the shoes aren't worth fighting over in the scheme of things (you'd much rather focus your attention on getting her to stop swearing in the house), and you'll turn to acceptance of the shoes, which will hopefully decrease the tension in the house. You may not accomplish the goal of *shoes put away*, but you'll be effective in improving your relationship with your daughter.

So what's the key to being more effective?

Put your rational wise mind in charge. Sure, your kid has your teeth on edge and every nerve jangling, but you know that if you allow your emotions to take over, someone (or both of you) will end up in tears.

Think effectively: identify your goals and objectives before you act, considering the long- and short-term impact of your actions, and focus on those goals throughout. (Remember your pros and cons skill? This is where those short-term versus long-term effects come in handy.) Keep your eye on the prize! You'll need to continually assess if your techniques are working or if they need to be adjusted; it may take several tries or, at times, help from an outside source.

AN "EFFECTIVELY" EXERCISE

Choose a battle that you've fought countless times with your child. It can be the tiniest (he leaves his cereal bowl on the table every...single... morning) or the more pressing (she yells, hits, and slams doors when she doesn't get what she wants).

Vividly replay the latest interaction in your head. Allow yourself to experience your thoughts and feelings as you recall the details. Next, practice your "cope ahead" skill from chapter 3: think of a more effective way to resolve the situation (or communicate) and imagine yourself carrying it out.

When you review that interaction, ask yourself:

- Was I effective?

- Did I get stuck on principle or did I focus on my goal?

- Did I consider the big picture and the whole situation?

- Was I realistic about my child and his capabilities?

- Was I willing to consider alternative actions and ways of thinking in the heat of the moment?

- Would it have been better if I hadn't responded?

- Did I behave like the parent I want to be?

Based on your (honest!) answers, you'll be able to begin formulating a strategy to handle it more effectively next time.

Mindfulness in Action

Many people—not just parents—find it helpful to adopt a mantra to help them focus, center, and calm the mind. While you may be tempted to try something like *only four more hours until bedtime* (and nobody can blame you for that!), find a phrase that will effectively soothe your heightened emotions.

Here are some suggestions:

Just this moment, just this breath, just this step. This is helpful when you want to stay mindful and present in the moment, especially in situations when you feel emotionally overwhelmed or consumed with worry.

Everything is as it should be. This is helpful when "should" and judgmental thoughts arise.

Do what works. This is helpful when you're getting stuck on what's "right" or having a hard time being effective.

Once you've found the mantra that works for you, write it down on an index card or sticky note (or set an alarm on your phone) and put it somewhere that you'll see it regularly. Practice saying it a few times to yourself every day (during calm times, too) until it becomes part of you.

Beyond mantras, there are mindfulness exercises that can help you center yourself throughout the day:

- Pay attention to your breathing. Put your hands on your belly and focus on the movement as you breathe in and out.

- Sit on a chair with your back straight and your hands in your lap. (Close your eyes if you tend to get visually distracted.) Notice and count your breaths: *inhale, 1; exhale, 2; inhale, 3; exhale, 4*…all the way to 10, and then start again from 1. If you get distracted, don't worry; just start again from 1.

- Be mindful of the sounds surrounding you: the hiss of the iron, the birds outside, the muted rumbling of traffic.

- Have a mindful treat. Brew a cup of tea or coffee or choose an individually wrapped chocolate, immersing yourself in the experience. Pay attention to the sounds of the kettle, the feel of the foil as you unwrap the chocolate, the aroma of your drink, the textures and flavors on your tongue and in your throat.

- Take a few minutes to center yourself before your kids walk in the door from school, before you walk out of your room into the morning fray, or before you sit down for a heart-to-heart with your hormone-crazed teen. Count your breaths to get yourself into the moment: *inhale, 1; exhale, 2; inhale, 3; exhale, 4…* Throw in your mantra for extra soothing power once your breathing regulates.

- Emotions taking over? Give yourself a time-out. Step out of the room (emergency bathroom break!) and observe your emotions (without judging yourself), paying attention as your emotion rises and falls as you breathe steadily. (In DBT, this is known as the "wave skill"—surf the emotion, riding the wave as it swells and breaks.)

- When an important concern enters your mind at an inopportune moment, don't focus on it—and don't push it away, either. Tell yourself that you will think about it at a predetermined time, then let go of it for the time being. (Write it down if you're afraid you'll forget.) Scheduling a time to focus on those concerns will help you be more present without neglecting the importance of the thought.

- Practice mindfulness with your children. Color with them, blow bubbles, take a walk and pay attention to the leaves crunching underfoot. Savor those moments together! Bonus: you'll be modeling mindfulness, which you know is a valuable skill, for them.

Rate your mindfulness (*On a scale of 0–10, how present am I in this moment?*) before beginning the exercise and again after you've completed it. See the difference?

Don't reserve these exercises for times of heightened emotion only. While they're definitely useful in daily parenting challenges, practicing these mini-meditations during everyday moments can help you become more centered and present in general. Research shows that regular mindfulness practice has numerous positive effects on the brain and body, and it can help you be calmer and more aware overall (Taren et al. 2015; Kabat-Zinn et al. 1998). Take those few minutes—they go a long way!

Ready to see what mindfulness looks like in everyday life?

This scene (or some version of it) may be familiar to you:

> It's Sunday morning, and the kids are sprawled out in their pajamas, watching cartoons. Mom is making pancakes as a treat and coordinating ballet carpool in a group chat on her phone. She walks into the living room to ask the kids—eleven-year-old Spencer, eight-year-old Sophia, and five-year-old Jack—if they want chocolate chips, entering just in time to see Spencer shove Sophia roughly.

Mom:	Spencer! What was that all about?
Spencer:	She hit me first! She keeps hogging the remote and switching back to girly shows!
Sophia:	That is so not true, you are such a liar! Mom, he's being so mean to me!
Mom:	Spencer, that is absolutely unacceptable. What kind of eleven-year-old hits his little sister? You should know better! You're being a bully!
Spencer:	But Mom—
Mom:	But nothing! You apologize to your sister right now or no more TV for today. I'm disappointed in your behavior.
Spencer:	I'm not apologizing! She's the one who's wrong! She should be punished, not me!
Mom:	Spencer, I saw you push her! Apologize or you'll lose privileges.
Spencer:	(*aggressively*) Fine. Sorry. Are you happy now? (*stomps out of the room and slams the door, while yelling about how everyone hates him and he wishes he could live somewhere else*)
Sophia:	(*smirks and changes the channel to her favorite "girly" show*) Mom, can I have syrup on my pancakes?

Where did this situation go wrong? Let us count the ways...

1. Mom is (understandably) distracted and stressed by the hectic Sunday schedule and the pinging of her phone (she doesn't want to get stuck with driving again this week!). She's not fully present in the moment.

   Missing mindfulness skills: One-mindfully, Participate

   The result: Spencer (understandably) feels that Mom isn't giving the situation her full attention, and Mom fails to notice important details.

2. Mom walks into the room in the middle of the situation and misses the part when Sophia *did* hit Spencer (and tease him, too). She immediately sizes up the situation and comes to the conclusion that Spencer started it, as he usually does.

   Missing mindfulness skills: Observe, Nonjudgmentally

   The result: Mom goes straight to interpreting (without having all the facts) rather than observing, mistaking her assumptions for facts. Spencer feels misunderstood, unheard, and resentful of his sister; he feels unmotivated to act appropriately because Mom always thinks it's his fault anyway.

3. Mom gets upset with Spencer based on his history and immediately launches into fix-it mode.

   Missing mindfulness skill: Observe

   The result: Spencer is automatically on the defensive. (Had Mom observed her own feelings and reactions, she would have noticed her urge to attack. She may have been aware enough to take a step back and assess her own emotional state before responding, avoiding this result.)

4. Mom labels Spencer's behavior as unacceptable, bullying, and age-inappropriate ("he should know better").

   Missing mindfulness skill: Nonjudgmentally

   The result: Spencer feels judged and thinks that his mother views him as immature, always wrong, and a bully.

5. Mom threatens Spencer to get him to apologize, which has the desired result (an apology) but without real, long-term effects.

   Missing mindfulness skill: Effectively

   The result: Spencer apologizes, but not sincerely, and learns that sincerity is not as important as the word "sorry." He leaves the encounter feeling wronged (and rightfully so), without any real consequence for shoving and without constructive change.

In short, all that comes out of this interaction are a lot of hurt feelings, stress, and guilt. Sophia, who's gotten away scot-free and is feeling triumphant and invincible, has learned that she can repeat that behavior and her brother will get punished instead of her.

With mindfulness, the result can be very different.

Take 2: with mindfulness skills…

Let's review. Mom walks into the room to catch Spencer shoving Sophia.

Mom:	(*takes a deep breath, turns off the stove, puts down the phone, and speaks in a neutral tone*) Hey guys, what's going on here? I see you using your hands.
	[*Mom notices (Observe) that she's feeling upset and takes a moment to calm herself before proceeding (One-mindfully). She puts away distractions so that she can focus on the situation and Describes the facts.*]
Spencer:	She hit me! I told her to give back the remote. She keeps hogging it and switching back to girly shows!
Sophia:	That is so not true, you are such a liar! Mom, he's being so mean to me! You hurt me! (*sticks out her tongue at Spencer*)
Mom:	Okay, everyone take a breath and calm down. I want to hear exactly what happened so that we can discuss this properly.
	[*Mom takes a moment (One-mindfully) to calm the kids— and herself—and listen to both of them so that she can consider all the details.*]
Spencer:	We agreed on a show, but as soon as she got bored she stole the remote and started changing the channel.
Sophia:	But then you called me a brat!
Spencer:	Well, yeah, you were being a brat.

Mom:　　Spencer, let's stick to the facts here, no name-calling. What happened next?

[Mom steers the conversation back on track, avoiding a digression and further fighting. She teaches and models Describing Nonjudgmentally.]

Spencer:　　Then she hit me! It really hurt. So I pushed her, and that's when you came in.

Mom:　　Sophia, let me hear your side now.

[Mom remains neutral and Nonjudgmental while gathering the details; she Observes and stays present, One-mindfully, in the moment.]

Sophia:　　He hurt my feelings! I wanted to watch something else! So I guess I hit him. But he pushed me!

Mom:　　You both hurt each other. We don't use our hands when we feel hurt in this house. Let's figure out a solution that will satisfy both of you. How do you guys think we can solve this problem of each of you wanting something different?

[Mom Participates, clearly Describing the situation to Effectively find a solution.]

Spencer:　　We picked a show together. I think we should go back to that one.

Sophia:　　But that one's boring. I'll go eat my pancakes, but only if you promise to let me watch my show when I'm done.

Mom:　　That sounds like a great idea. I'm proud of you both for sorting that out maturely. We have enough time for both of you to pick a show before we have to leave. Now, who wants chocolate chips?

They may not have apologized to each other, but they've learned a valuable lesson in getting along, problem solving, and compromising. And Mom never lost her cool, so she's feeling pretty good about herself. It's a win-win!

Roadblocks to Mindfulness

Mindfulness tends to be misunderstood. Like many people, you may have deep-seated beliefs that stand in the way of your practicing it effectively. This table shows some common roadblocks, or beliefs about mindfulness, and some different ways to think about or approach them. These "roadblocks" and "detours" are also available to download and print at http://www.newharbinger.com/46868 (see Chapter 4 Roadblock Cards) to serve as regular reminders.

Roadblock (assumption or belief)	Detour (the solution)
Mindfulness is for those crunchy yoga types, not me!	Mindfulness is for everyone, especially for parents—and it's very different from sitting in the lotus position and saying "om."
I have no time to waste on sitting around and meditating.	Try incorporating just a few minutes of mindfulness into your day—they don't even have to be all at once, and they can be incorporated into everyday tasks.
I need to multitask—it's the only way I can get everything done! I'm a parent; I don't have a lot of time on my hands.	Spend a few days consciously *not* multitasking and recognize the difference in your level of efficiency and accuracy. Studies show that multitasking does not actually save time!
It's too hard not to be judgmental. I've been doing this all my life, I'm a great judge of character, and I'm usually right on target!	This tendency can be really difficult to overcome! Start by labeling and noticing your judgments without trying to change them.
Every time I try to be mindful, my mind just wanders all over the place. I'm not cut out for this.	A wandering mind is perfectly natural and is actually part of the mindfulness process! Keep reining in your wandering thoughts and gently redirecting them; you will train your brain over time.

After reading this chapter, you hopefully have a better understanding of what mindfulness is, the "what" and "how" skills involved in mindfulness, and, most importantly, how to put them into action. Even if you're a mindfulness skeptic, give it a try—the benefits are boundless. With mindfulness, you'll be more productive, effective, attentive, flexible, understanding, accepting, and in control of yourself. At the same time, you'll be less stressed, reactive, combative, tense, rigid, unhappy, and frustrated. And that's a surefire recipe for improved relationships in all areas of life—and especially in parenting! In the next chapter we'll look at another important parenting skill: validation.

CHAPTER 5

Validation: The Relationship Booster

Validation.

It's one of those hotly debated concepts: some will assert that an overload of validation is what's destroying the "participation trophy" generation, while others will just as confidently say that validation is the key to emotional health.

Either extreme view is anti-dialectic. Validation—when properly defined and executed—is indeed a central and crucial ingredient in healthy, happy relationships and in raising confident, balanced children, especially those who have difficulty regulating their emotions. However, much of what's casually bandied about as "validation" may actually be detrimental.

So how do you go about validating effectively? How do you know if you're doing it right or not?

In this chapter, you'll learn the answers to these questions:

- What is (and isn't) validation?

- What is invalidation?

- Why is validation important?

- When, what, and how do I validate effectively?

- How can I overcome obstacles to validation?

What Is Validation?

Essentially, validation communicates to your child that you understand her and that you want to connect and identify with her feelings, thoughts, and actions.

Validation in parenting is...

...working to understand your child's point of view.

Test this concept: Think of a song and drum out the beat. Ask a friend, spouse, or child to guess the song. Chances are, the observer will not be able to name the tune, even though it's so clear to you! Recognize that even if a concept or perspective is clear and logical in your mind, your child may not have that same clarity. (Similarly, your child's perspective makes sense to him...even if you can't fathom it!)

...acknowledging that there is a cause for your child's behavior and emotions.

Find the kernel of truth—the causes behind your child's behavior, even if it seems ludicrous to you—and acknowledge it in your mind. Write down all possible causes, no matter how ridiculous they may seem, and then highlight which one(s) are most likely driving your child's behavior. If you cannot find a kernel of truth, acknowledge that there *is* one, even if you don't know what it is.

...making sense of your child's thoughts, actions, and feelings based on past and present events and circumstances.

Consider your child's fears, experiences, personality, and other circumstances; try to put yourself in her place or recall times when you experienced something similar. Ask yourself: *Was I capable of this task (paying attention to homework for extended periods of time, keeping quiet while Mom talked on the phone, sitting at the dinner table...) at this age? What was I sensitive about when I was a child/teen? How did it feel when my parents showed me that they understood what I was feeling?*

...focusing on the big picture.

Look beyond the situation at hand. You don't know what you can't see (remember your Observe skill); your child may have experienced an unpleasant interaction with a friend or teacher today, may be preoccupied with a secret, may be upset because you forgot to pack his favorite snack like you promised... or may simply be in a mood without any idea why.

This is important, especially for all those validation skeptics out there: validation does *not* mean that you agree or approve of the behavior, emotion, action, or sentiment expressed by your child. You can validate your child and his point of view without agreeing with or approving of it.

What Is Invalidation?

Even the most well-intentioned, loving, tuned-in parent occasionally engages in invalidation—intentionally or unintentionally.

Invalidation can be manifested verbally, behaviorally, or physically, through words, actions, facial expressions, and body language.

Invalidation sounds like this:

- "Yes, but…"

- "It's not such a big deal."

- "This situation should not have made you so upset/anxious/frustrated/afraid."

- "Get your chin up; everything will be fine."

- "Can't you act your age?"

- "Your sister never behaved like this."

- "I would never have gotten away with talking to my father like that."

- "You're lucky I put up with this nonsense."

- "We need to get you some serious help; this is not normal."

Invalidation looks like this:

- Rushing your child through her story or interrupting her.

- Not believing your child.

- Trying to distract your child from the issue at hand.

- Rolling your eyes, looking annoyed, squirming (even if you think your child's not watching!); body language speaks louder than words!

Invalidation is harmful in that it has the opposite effects of validation: it often leaves the child feeling misunderstood, upset, and not any closer to a solution. This is particularly common in children who have difficulty with emotional regulation: if you are more even-keeled, you probably *didn't* act like this, so it's hard for you to relate. In reality, your child's emotionally dysregulated behavior *isn't* "the norm."

However, invalidation is actually important at times (that's dialectics for you—virtually everything can be effective in the right situation). When you provide corrective feedback to your child, that feedback can invalidate the child's thoughts and feelings, which is sometimes necessary for growth and change.

Necessary invalidation may sound like this:

- "I know you may feel like I'm angry at you. I want you to know that I'm not."

- "I can see why you might think I don't care about you, but that's very far from the truth!"

- "No, I didn't let your brother do that when he was your age."

- "It may seem like everyone in your class gets to stay up later than you do. I checked with a bunch of other parents and many kids have the same bedtime as you."

Why Is Validation Important?

Marsha Linehan, who developed DBT, asserts that a child's ability to regulate his emotions depends directly on emotional validation (Linehan 1993). For kids who struggle with their emotions—whether it's due to a diagnosis like DMDD or ADHD or simply heightened sensitivity—validation is an absolute must for their emotional health.

A child who experiences extreme emotion in an invalidating environment learns that his displays of emotion are unjustified and that he should be able to "deal with" his emotions on his own. This leads the child to stifle his emotions continually until they boil over in explosions of emotion. On the other hand, when his emotions are validated, he learns to identify, understand, and tolerate those emotions, which helps him (eventually) learn to regulate his emotions in a healthy manner and to problem solve effectively once his emotions are in check.

Think about a time when you felt strongly about something and somebody discounted your feelings. Maybe you were excited about a childhood trip or a new toy until a sibling or friend deemed it "babyish"; perhaps it was when you submitted a complaint at work and your boss brushed it off; or it could have been when you told your spouse that you were upset about a friend's comment and she dismissed your feelings.

Did that experience give you the warm-and-fuzzies for the other person? Did you start second-guessing your (very real) concerns or emotions? Did it help you work through your feelings? Did you feel enthusiastic or motivated to find a solution?

Chances are the interaction left you feeling misunderstood, hurt, distant from the other party, and unmotivated.

That's the power of validation.

Below we'll consider some compelling reasons to validate.

Improve Communication and Emotion Regulation

Validation communicates to your child that you understand him and that his feelings make sense (even if you don't agree with them). Rather than sensing that his feelings are wrong, stupid, or too intense, validation helps your child identify, make sense of, and feel secure in his emotions, which enhances his self-respect and familiarity with his own emotions. Once he names the emotion (or you help him name his emotion), he can regulate it more easily. When he feels understood, he'll no longer feel the need to express his emotion (e.g., fury, sadness, frustration) quite as strongly.

One of the essential functions of emotion is to communicate your feelings to others; once you validate your child, that function has been effectively completed, and the intensity of the emotion decreases. Validation increases the ability to clearly communicate feelings and provide feedback during difficult times, a valuable skill for every child and adult to use throughout life's challenges.

As part of a study (Mendolia and Kleck, 1993), college students were shown a traumatic video and asked to describe their reactions. One group was given free rein to express their feelings, while the other was told to describe the facts only. The "feelings group" experienced stronger emotion (and physiological effects) than the "facts group" when describing the video.

Both groups viewed the video again forty-eight hours later. This time, both were allowed to describe the facts and their feelings. The feelings group was considerably less emotional than the original facts group when describing the video for the second time. The very act of communicating their feelings helped them deal with the disturbing images.

When we recognize and label our emotions, we initially feel them more intensely. Over time, describing and communicating emotions helps us self-regulate more effectively.

Decrease Conflict

Validation strengthens relationships by increasing both parties' positive feelings toward each other and decreasing anger and intensity during conflict. When your child sees that you understand her, she will be able to move forward rather than harping on "You don't understand me!" Feeling understood will quiet the intensity of her emotion and enable her to work through the problem more calmly.

Validating often defuses an emotion before it has a chance to escalate. Imagine this: you tell your child that you'll take him out at 5:30 to pick up his favorite sushi for dinner. He runs off to play with his friends and comes back after the designated time, just as you're all sitting down to eat. He immediately protests that you promised him sushi. If you launch straight into explanations about how he should've come back on time and now it's too late, but he can have sushi tomorrow, he'll likely get more upset, spiraling into an argument. If you acknowledge his disappointment, it'll take the wind out of his sails and allow him to be more receptive to your explanation and solution.

Validation acknowledges the truth and verifies the facts on both sides, allowing both parties to reach a "baseline" of sorts; it gets everyone on the same page before attempting to solve the problem.

Increase Motivation

Validation motivates us to continue working toward our goals; when we're in a positive frame of mind and feel understood, we're less likely to give up. A study on willpower (Baumeister et al. 1998) demonstrated the effect of positive feelings on persistence. Two groups of subjects were exposed to chocolatey smells and delicious-looking treats. After exposure, one group was allowed to eat the tempting chocolates while the other was given radishes. Afterward, both groups were given a persistence-testing puzzle to solve. The disappointed radish-eating group gave up faster and made far fewer attempts to solve the puzzle. The group whose chocolate cravings were indulged spent more than twice as long as the radish group.

Create a Better Mindset

Finally, validation makes us feel understood and supported, which results in a more positive mindset. Those feel-good messages can increase willpower and persistence, so we'll try harder for longer. In the chocolate versus radish study, the sweets group went into the test buoyed and motivated by their positive feelings; they then persisted far longer than the radish group.

Your "uncontrollable" child is struggling. It's difficult for him to cope with daily challenges and emotions, and he expends a lot of energy on keeping himself in check. Providing validation can help him achieve a positive state of mind, empowering him to keep trying.

Validation is considered an acceptance strategy; its purpose is to help you understand the situation rather than change it, and it enables both you and your child to move on to effective problem solving by quieting the atmosphere and creating a shared sense of awareness.

While validation is important for every child, it's exceptionally crucial for children who tend to react strongly. When dysregulated children are not validated, their already intense emotions intensify further and they become impulsive and reactive in response. This often continues until they get a response, which reinforces the dysregulation. These children's innate heightened sensitivity causes them to pick up on your emotions nearly instantaneously, sometimes even before you become aware of those emotions! Every facial expression, every gesture, every change in the tone of your voice is interpreted and experienced as invalidation.

Validation in Action

Now for the real work: the art of proper validation.

There are two main approaches to express validation: verbal validation and functional (behavioral) validation.

Verbal validation is validating with words; it sounds like this:

- "You must be so upset!"

- "That really is disappointing."

- "It makes sense that you're upset about this; I was upset when something similar happened to me."

- "You probably felt really embarrassed when the teacher yelled at you!"

Functional validation, also known as behavioral validation, is validating with actions and behaviors; it's often more powerful than verbal validation. It looks like this:

- Handing your crying child a tissue

- Putting your arm around her shoulder

- Pouring a cold cup of water for a flushed, sweaty child

- Calling the teacher about an unfair situation

- Telling one child to stop bothering his sibling

- Helping your child study for an important exam

- Brainstorming solutions to deal with a bully

This type of validation shows—in actions that, as the cliché goes, speak louder than words—that you understand your child and feel what she's feeling. Imagine coming across a person hanging out the window of a burning building. Technically, you can verbally validate him ("You must be so hot and so scared!"), but calling the fire department or directing him to the fire escape will communicate your empathy clearly and effectively!

What to Validate

It can be extremely difficult to validate, especially when you can't relate to or don't agree with the emotion, thought, or behavior. It's important to *validate the valid, not the invalid.* In other words, even if the sentiment is invalid, the emotion may be very valid. While the intensity of the emotion may not be justified under the circumstances, it can still be understandable based on previous experiences.

Imagine this: your teen comes home crying that she flunked a test—the test that you *know* she didn't study for—and you're tempted to forgo the validation and remind her about how she goofed off instead of studying. (Don't worry—she knows that she messed up and that it's her fault that she failed; she doesn't need your reminder.)

Validate *the valid*: her feelings of anger and disappointment (say: "It sounds like you're really upset about that grade").

Don't validate *the invalid*: the fact that she didn't study (don't say: "It makes sense that you flunked; I bet it was a really hard test").

Find the valid kernel of truth in every interaction and validate that. To better understand this skill, let's look at some examples of invalidating and validating responses.

Your child says, "Ms. Patterson is the worst teacher ever!"

Invalidating response: "You're right, she's the worst!" (Alternatively: "C'mon, she's not that bad.")

Validating response: "It sounds like you're really not enjoying Mrs. Patterson's class… You were happier with Mr. Johnson last year, weren't you?"

Your child says, "You give him whatever he wants and I never get anything!"

Invalidating response: "No, I give you all what you need. Remember when you got candy last week and he didn't? Fair doesn't mean equal."

Validating response: "I can see that you're feeling frustrated and I understand why you would think it's not fair."

Your child says, "My teacher yelled at me for coming a minute after the bell. It wasn't my fault! I'm mortified! He's going to fail me!"

Invalidating response: "It's not so embarrassing; it happens all the time. I bet your classmates forgot about it already. I'm sure she didn't scream at you. Don't you think you're being a little too sensitive? Just try harder to come on time from now on."

Validating response: "That must have been embarrassing. I remember that feeling of trying to sneak in after the bell rang!"

Your child says, "I studied for that test for hours and hours, and I only got an 88! Everyone else got a higher grade."

Invalidating response: "Eighty-eight is a great grade; don't worry about it! You've been doing so well all year, it won't affect your GPA. And I'm sure some other kids did worse than that."

Validating response: "That's disappointing! You really did study hard."

Your child says, "She messed everything up in our room again! I can't stand sharing a room with a slob! Why can't I have my own room like every normal teenager instead of sharing?"

Invalidating response: "Relax, it's not such a big deal. We don't have enough room for you to have your own. And don't call your sister names. She just left a couple of things on the floor. You've never seen what a real slob looks like!"

Validating response: "It can be hard to share a room with your sister. I'll have a talk with her about keeping her stuff on her side of the room."

Your child says, "You hate me!"

> **Invalidating response:** "I could never hate you! What a ridiculous thing to say!"

> **Validating response:** "I'm sorry that you feel like I hate you when I really love you."

Your child says, "I hate you!"

> **Invalidating response:** "You do not hate me; you're just saying that because you're angry."

> **Validating response:** "You're very angry about this. Let's discuss it when you feel calmer."

When Not to Validate

Don't forget your dialectics; overvalidating can be ineffective as well, so keep it balanced! When a child is overly dysregulated and experiencing extremely heightened emotion or is stuck in his current mindset, he may need some time to calm down before he's ready to benefit from validation. Additionally, when a child is actively engaging in an aggressive or inappropriate behavior, validation may serve as a reinforcer. In that situation, a change skill such as extinction (which we'll address in chapter 7) may be more effective. Validation may also be ineffective in an overly stimulating or noisy environment, where your words of validation may be overpowered by the surrounding distractions. Another issue to consider is whether your child will be embarrassed if you validate her in front of others (family, friends, even strangers). If so, move to a quieter place or continue the discussion at a different time. And finally, if your skill use does not seem to be effective, quit while you're ahead! You can always revisit the conversation later.

How to Validate

Validation skills are handy for every relationship. You can use them with any child (not only the emotionally sensitive or dysregulated child), with your spouse, with your sister-in-law, or with your boss.

There are six levels of validation, or six techniques to employ to effectively help your child feel validated. Don't worry about hitting each level every time you validate; you don't need to use them all or use them in order. Practice one level at a time to avoid getting overwhelmed.

The six levels are:

1. **Be present.** Maintain eye contact with your child and show interest in his story or complaint—verbally and nonverbally. Examples of this are nodding along, being mindful of your facial expressions, and saying "uh-huh" or "I see" at appropriate intervals. Listen attentively and actively, and reduce distractions: put away your phone, tell a different child to wait, tell the child in question that you have to continue stirring dinner but that you are listening.

2. **Reflect without judgment.** Repeat the facts ("So you're saying that everyone else is going to the movie at 4:30?") and listen to your child—she may correct you if you get it wrong. Watch your tone for judgmental quality, unnatural speech, or sarcasm. Avoid "but," which dismisses the first part of the sentence ("I know you're upset, but that behavior is not okay" or "I understand that you don't want to go, but the bus is coming right now"). Replace "but" with "and" or "at the same time."

3. **Read your child's mind.** Not literally! Use a word to describe your child's emotion ("I see that you're upset"). Examine your child for clues about what he's really feeling and take an educated guess ("I can't take you to the store right now because I have to finish cooking dinner; you must feel disappointed!"). Again, listen to your child's response; you may have the wrong guess, and that's okay—be open to corrections. When you show your child that you "get" him, it removes some of the fuel from his fired-up emotions and allows you to come to a solution calmly; it also helps him name and make sense of his emotions.

4. **Communicate understanding based on the past.** Convey to your child that her behavior/thought/emotion makes sense in light of previous events, experiences, and circumstances ("After what happened there last time, I can understand why you don't want to go back!"). Don't gloss over experiences that may have been upsetting to your child. You may think that doing so will help her "get over it," but she is actually more likely to get over it if she feels that her reaction is valid. You may also think that putting a positive spin on the experience ("Look, the scrape that you got from falling off the monkey bars is all

better now!") will help your child move on, but validating it ("Yes, that really did hurt and it was scary; should I hold onto your legs this time?") will be more effective.

5. **Validate based on the present.** Communicate to your child that his behavior/thought/emotion makes sense in terms of present events and the way that most people would react to current circumstances. This is the "heart" of validation—it normalizes your child's reaction and makes him feel understood. If your child is antsy about leaving on a trip or outing, don't say, "Would you relax already? We're leaving in three minutes, just be patient!" A more effective approach that will keep everyone's nerves under control would be "I know, you're so excited, it's hard to wait for a few minutes! Maybe you can help me pack up the snacks so that we can get on the road faster."

6. **Be radically genuine.** Your child is no fool; he knows when you're sincere, so try to put yourself into his place before validating him. And be careful not to patronize! Watch your tone and body language. If you're feeling unnatural and scripted, your child will pick up on that; be as genuine as possible. Don't worry—it may be stiff or awkward at first, but with practice, validation will begin to come naturally to you!

It can help to *cope ahead* when you start working on validation. Rehearse in front of a mirror (yes, really!) or script your conversation beforehand (every bit of practice helps you be more genuine).

When you start using the levels of validation, evaluate yourself to see which level challenges you the most. Review and rewrite a conversation that went poorly; evaluate it to see how you could have used your skills. Realize that "results" are not instantaneous. Take time to ensure that your child feels understood before continuing the conversation or explaining your reasoning or perspective. Moving on to problem solving or explanations too quickly may invalidate the validation.

Remember: validation does not necessarily mean agreeing with or approving of your child's actions or feelings, but rather understanding her motivation.

If you're not sure what to do—and that's common, especially with kids who may have a hard time expressing themselves—ask!

- "How can I be most helpful right now? Do you want advice or do you just want me to hear you out?"

- "I want to understand why you're so upset about this. Let's keep talking so that I can really get it."

- "I'm not sure I totally understand what happened and what's bothering you. Here's a cup of water. Can we try again?"

There are times when you'll do everything right and still not have any significant effect on your child's emotional state. A personal example: My son was leaving for overnight camp for the very first time. He was understandably nervous, and I employed all of my validation techniques to help him out. He only felt truly validated once he met up with a friend who was in the same situation and experiencing the same nerves. His friend was able to validate him in ways that I wasn't, simply because he was a peer in the same stage of life and not his old social-worker dad!

Take a moment to try out your validation skills in an all-too-common scenario: It's nearly the end of the morning rush. The kids are eating breakfast, backpacks are packed, and Mom is attempting to get herself ready so that she can be out the door on time. The bus will be in front of the house in ten minutes.

That's when nine-year-old Samantha chooses to make her declaration. (Kids tend to have impeccable timing, don't they?)

Samantha: (*scowling*) I am *not* going to school today.

Mom: Honey, the bus will be here in ten minutes. I'm sure you'll have a great day; you have art class today! Finish your cereal.

[*Mom is understandably rushing and tries to distract Samantha without trying to hear her perspective.*]

Samantha: (*tearing up*) I don't care about art class; I can finish my painting at home. Nobody likes me. I hate school! I'm not going!

Mom: Sam, sweetheart, don't be silly, you have lots of friends! What about Emma? And Charlotte? And Liam? You play with them all the time.

[*Mom downplays Samantha's feelings and tries to argue logically against her statement.*]

Samantha: No! Everyone's mean to me! They make fun of me! I am not going back to school ever!

Mom: (*packing lunches*) Jake, clear off your bowl and go get your shoes on. Samantha, I think you're overreacting a little. We'll talk about this after school. I know you're having a hard time, but this is not the time to take care of it. I'm going to be late for work.

> [*Mom invalidates Samantha's reaction; she is dividing her attention between lunches and the other kids rather than focusing on the matter at hand, which leads to Samantha's feeling misunderstood, unheard, and unimportant.*]

Samantha: (*sullenly*) You don't care about me, you only care about work. I'm going to have a horrible day. Why can't you understand me?

Mom: (*trying to contain her impatience*) I understand you just fine, I need *you* to understand that now is not a good time to deal with this. Here's a cookie. Take your backpack, the bus is here! I love you!

> [*Mom continues to contradict Samantha's thoughts, emotions, and statements without addressing or validating them. She attempts to make Samantha feel better with a totally unrelated offer of a cookie to get her to stop feeling or expressing this emotion.*]

Samantha: (*stomps out of the house in tears*)

Mom: (*on the verge of tears herself*)

How can Mom handle this properly and still manage to get the kids off to school (and herself off to work) on time? She doesn't need superpowers—just some strategic validation skills.

Samantha: (*scowling*) I am *not* going to school today.

Mom: (*looks Samantha in the eye*) What's going on?

> [*Validation level: 1. Mom gives Samantha her full attention and asks for her viewpoint.*]

Samantha: (*tearing up*) Nobody likes me. The other kids are so mean to me! I hate school! I'm not going!

Mom: (*putting her arm around Samantha*) Oh, Sam, I know, those kids said some really mean things to you yesterday. That makes you want to stay home from school. I can only imagine how hurt you must feel.

[Validation levels: 2, 3. Mom reflects nonjudgmentally, names Samantha's emotion, and tells her why her feelings make sense based on her experiences.]

Samantha: (*crying*) They are! They're so mean! I don't want to see them again!

[Samantha's emotions intensify briefly, which is an expected reaction.]

Mom: I know, and they were pretty nasty at summer camp too. I'm pretty upset myself. I have a call scheduled with Mrs. Gardner this morning to discuss it; we're going to take care of this problem right away. Also, I want you to remember that there are kids who are nice too—you said that you played with Emma and Liam yesterday, right? There is so much to like about you, because you're a really cool kid, and I know that Mrs. Gardner will help those girls see why you're so awesome.

[Validation levels: 4, 5. Mom empathizes with Samantha based on the past and present and shows that she is taking this seriously, beyond simple verbal validation.]

Samantha: (*sniffling*) I still don't want to go.

Mom: I get that, sweetheart. I know you don't want to get on the bus right now. At the same time, school is a must. We will talk about this more when you get home. C'mon, I'll help you pack up your backpack. You can take an extra snack to share with Charlotte.

[Validation levels: 5, 6. Mom continues to show that she genuinely understands Samantha and shows her that her feelings are normal even as she helps her move forward.]

Samantha: I guess I can sit with Charlotte.

Mom: That's my strong girl! I'm rooting for you! Let's do this! Have a great day, and remember, I'm going to talk to Mrs. Gardner, so if anything comes up you can talk to her too.

[Validation level: 6. Mom verbally and functionally validates Samantha again.]

Samantha: Okay.

And off she goes, still nervous and a bit teary, but ready to face the day—and Mom's feeling pretty good about herself, too.

Roadblocks to Validation

The road to effectively validating your child is frequently blocked by various factors that lead to invalidation. The most common roadblocks to validation, and the detours (solutions), are shown below. You can also download the Chapter 5 Roadblock Cards from http://www.newharbinger.com/46868.

Roadblock (the statement)	Detour (the solution)
This is not right! *She should not react like this!*	Focus on being effective and on what is rather than what "should" be.
I can't validate. I don't know how. It's too awkward.	Practice the validation skills in this chapter! It may be awkward at first, but it will become easier with time and practice.
How am I supposed to know if this behavior is valid in the first place or if I'm validating something invalid?	Do your homework: Read up on or research child development, societal norms, or other pertinent information. Learn as much as you can about your child's particular personality, diagnosis, and challenges.

Roadblock (the statement)	Detour (the solution)
I can't be bothered with this whole process! Why can't she just behave normally?	Practice self-care and mindfulness skills to get yourself into the frame of mind for effective validation.
Come on, it's never going to work on this kid. Oh, he needs validation? Is that all? Getting validated is the least of his problems!	Practice validation skills with an open mind and assess their effectiveness on a regular basis.
How can I validate when her point of view is totally skewed?	Practice mindfulness and dialectical skills; look for the kernel of truth.
If I say, "You must be scared," it will suddenly occur to him to be scared! I don't want to put ideas in his head.	Validate the valid, not the invalid; when executed properly, validation will help the child process emotions—not manufacture them.
If she'd just listen to me, she'd see that it's so easy to fix the problem rather than blow it out of proportion!	When a child is distressed, that's not a good time to try solving the problem; validation will help her calm down so that she can focus on effective solutions. (And at times, validation is all that's needed to regulate the problematic emotion!)
There is no way I would have ever spoken to my father like that! He's just trying to be difficult.	Practice mindfulness skills to work on reducing and reframing judgmental thoughts.
I just can't deal with this! She pushes all my buttons and I'm supposed to think about her feelings?	Before attempting validation, validate your own emotions by giving yourself some space to regulate, self-soothe, and respond calmly to your own problematic thinking patterns.

Roadblock (the statement)	Detour (the solution)
He freaks out when I try to validate. It just doesn't work for him! He takes it as permission to do what he wants.	See "When *Not* to Validate"—your child may need time to calm down before he can be receptive to validation.
If I validate, it will just make the whole situation worse!	Try it out. You may see magic unfold!

Parenting a child with emotional regulation difficulties is hard; parents need validation, too! Give yourself a pat on the back for dealing with the challenges and seeking to improve your skills. It's normal to feel frustrated and upset when your child acts in ways that don't fit in with your expectations; it's normal to feel disappointed that your child is different; it's normal to feel embarrassed by your child's behavior; it's normal to feel sad that your child struggles in areas that other kids don't.

In this chapter you learned the benefits of validation for your child and how to use this skill. Take the time to practice your validation skills on yourself, too; it will help you be more present to validate your child effectively. Apply the six levels of validation to your own struggles and avoid judging and invalidating yourself, which can get in the way of accomplishing your long-term goals.

This concludes the chapters on acceptance strategies, though you'll find the concepts woven into the change-focused chapters as well. Next, we'll move on to the skills that will help you shape your child's behavior, starting with reinforcement.

CHAPTER 6

Reinforcement Strategies to Shape Your Child's Behavior

Give yourself a pat on the back! You've learned all about acceptance, including the necessary skills of mindfulness and validation, and you're (hopefully) feeling pretty confident about your new and improved parenting methods. *Acceptance is the key. Shower them with love.* When your child feels your acceptance, the whole atmosphere in the house will change.

And it's true. Your child may have looked at you suspiciously when you validated her the first few times, but—miracle of miracles—it has likely staved off many a tantrum. You may be finding it easier to relate to her, even when you're burning mad. And the little one has even started adopting your mindfulness mantras.

Go you!

At some point, though, you probably hit a snag.

Despite all of your acceptance and wholehearted love, he's still the little heathen that propelled you to pick up this book; she's still mouthing off at every opportunity; the house is still a testament to rages, tantrums, inherent uncontrollability.

C'mon, acceptance was supposed to work!

In fact, while acceptance is a critical parenting skill and definitely has its time and place, constant, unconditional, unlimited acceptance is not the be-all-end-all of parenting. An all-acceptance, totally positive approach is very rarely effective or healthy.

Every parent *wants* their child to feel loved and accepted, validated and understood, cared for and valued. At the same time, we also want them to be well behaved and compliant.

That's where the *change strategies* come in.

It's imperative to create a healthy balance of acceptance *and* change in order for your child to learn which behaviors are problematic and to adjust or replace them with new, more effective behaviors. This chapter, as well as the next two chapters, focuses on change; they'll equip you with an arsenal of practical, implementable strategies to effectively shape your child's behavior.

In this chapter, you'll learn:

- Change strategies for increasing your child's good behaviors

- Effective reinforcement techniques

- The difference between positive and negative reinforcement (spoiler: it's probably not what you think!)

- How and when to implement reinforcement

- How to overcome obstacles to reinforcement

Change strategies are your tools for success: they're techniques that will help you increase your child's good behaviors and decrease the problematic ones. As you learned in previous chapters, acceptance will help lay the groundwork for change; the techniques that you'll learn to shape behavior will complete the task for maximum effectiveness.

These change skills are not skills for you to teach to your child; they're skills for you to practice as you parent your child. The changes that you'll make in your parenting will consequently lead to behavioral changes in your child.

What Is Reinforcement?

Our brains are plastic.

No, not like the model brains you may have used in grade school. Scientists refer to the malleability of our brains as "neural plasticity": just as plastic is heated and molded into different shapes, our brains are shaped and changed by the happenings in our lives.

This pliability is what allows us to learn and adopt new behaviors.

When your child learns a behavior that you're not crazy about—like screaming to get what he wants—you want him to "unlearn" it as soon as possible. The trouble is, unlearning is not quite so simple, especially once the behavior becomes a habit. His brain develops an automatic response: the thought of *I want it* translates into *If I scream, Mom will give it to me*. And every time his screaming gets him what he wants, the *want → scream → get* connection in his head becomes a well-worn path.

Don't worry—that doesn't mean that he'll be doing it forever! It's entirely possible to replace it with a different behavior. While we can't just get rid of a brain pathway, we *can* overpower it with a new pathway.

The pathways in your child's brain are like physical paths through a forest. Some are smooth, while others are bumpy and uncharted. It's natural to choose the smoothest, easiest path; every time you walk that path, it becomes even smoother and easier to walk on. A rougher, less-traveled path will be more challenging to navigate, but as you continue to take that path, it will eventually smooth out.

That's what reinforcement does: it steers your child's brain down a new path. The terrain will be bumpy in the beginning, but as he learns and strengthens the new behavior, the path levels out and becomes the default. The old, easy path—the old habit—won't disappear entirely, but it will become overgrown and uneven from disuse.

Your child may revert to the old behavior on occasion, especially in the beginning (when his brain is used to heading down the old, smoother path). Over time, however, the newer behavior (asking nicely) will largely replace the old behavior (screaming) as the habitual, instinctive path.

When you reinforce the behavior that you want to introduce, encourage, or increase, you're setting up new connections in your child's brain, effectively rewiring his behavior. That's why it's important to reinforce the desired behavior (like helping out, asking nicely, finishing dinner, or doing homework) rather than the undesired behavior (like tantruming, screaming, fighting, or punching).

Done properly, reinforcement can translate to getting your kid to do what you want him to do—or to stop doing—by letting the reinforcer (AKA a reward) do the work.

Types of Reinforcement

Behavioral psychologist B. F. Skinner (1953) described two types of reinforcement: *positive reinforcement* and *negative reinforcement*, both of which are essential in shaping behavior and parenting effectively.

Now, the positive/negative terminology can get confusing. In everyday language, "positive" generally means "good" while "negative" usually indicates "bad": "It was a positive experience." "I got negative feedback." "You're always so cheerful and positive!" "He's giving off negative vibes here."

But in behavioral terms, positive and negative have different meanings.

Positive = adding something

Negative = removing or avoiding something

To shape your child's behavior with reinforcement, you'll attach an incentive or deterrent to the behavior that will affect your child's response. That incentive may be something that your child wants, like a reward or compliment (positive reinforcement) or something that he doesn't want, like not being able to go out and play (negative reinforcement).

So in that context, let's go a little deeper into what positive and negative reinforcement mean in this book.

Positive Reinforcement

Positive reinforcement is rewarding a desired behavior by adding a positive consequence. For example, your child gets extra screen time when she finishes her homework quickly. In general, this technique tends to be the gentlest behavior-shaping technique; it carries the smallest risk of negative emotions and strain on the parent-child relationship. As a matter of fact, it will likely increase positive feelings and mutual understanding in the parent-child relationship—and who wouldn't want more positivity?

Receiving positive reinforcement for a behavior makes your child want to perform that behavior again. It's like earning frequent flyer miles on your credit card: you're inclined to use that card for every purchase to save up toward your dream vacation.

Reinforcement can be as easy as positive interactions—a kind word, a smile, a high five—with your child. Executed properly, positive reinforcement will give your child the desire to repeat his behavior.

It's easy to overlook your child's good behavior (especially when you're trying to enjoy the moment before the next crisis hits), but it's important to be mindful and reinforce even the smallest bits of goodness, however few and far between they may be. When you reinforce the simple things—like putting his dirty clothes in the hamper instead of on the floor—he's likely to do it again.

Negative Reinforcement

The word "negative" can be deceiving sometimes. You might think that negative reinforcement means reinforcing behavior by introducing a negative consequence, but it doesn't. (That's actually known as "positive punishment," which you'll learn about in chapter 7.)

In actuality, negative reinforcement is a method that you can use to increase a behavior by introducing something that your child wants to avoid (a reinforcer). She will be motivated to perform the behavior in order to *avoid* or *get relief from* the unpleasant, undesired reinforcer. It's like that annoying beeping sound your car makes when you fail to put on your seatbelt—you find yourself buckling up (the behavior) to make the beeping (the reinforcer) stop, and eventually you'll belt in before it even starts to beep, avoiding the beeping completely.

Similarly, in parenting, negative reinforcement may be nagging your child to clean her room: she'll clean up just to make you stop.

Like positive reinforcement, negative reinforcement increases the probability that your child will repeat the behavior (because it provides relief from something she dislikes). So the next time you start nagging her to clean up, she will most likely do it faster to avoid your nagging.

Unlike positive reinforcement, negative reinforcement comes with a built-in penalty. A common example: "You can go play after you've finished cleaning your room." Playtime is postponed until the room is clean, so the faster the child cleans up, the more time he'll have to play.

Let's break it down.

- You want your child to clean his room, so you use reinforcement (postponing playtime) to increase the behavior (cleaning his room).

- You're not adding any reward (playtime is part of the normal routine), so it's not positive reinforcement.

- He needs to do something (clean his room) in order to avoid losing playtime. Remember, in behavioral terms, "negative" = avoiding.

Negative reinforcement is very powerful; nobody likes to feel uncomfortable. It's often what leads to destructive behaviors, such as alcoholism. People engage in harmful behaviors to "take the pain away"—and when it's effective, odds are they'll do it again.

In parenting, negative reinforcement—like positive reinforcement—is an important skill. Positive reinforcement focuses on changing and strengthening behavior in the future, whereas negative reinforcement is especially effective at changing behavior on short notice. (And so many parenting moments come with absolutely no notice!) When your child stands to lose something that he wants (or to get relief from something that he doesn't want), he'll likely be more inclined to behave the way you want him to.

Remember, don't let the word "negative" fool you; negative reinforcement can also be phrased positively, as this table shows:

Examples of Negative Reinforcement Phrases

Phrased Negatively (what not to say)	Phrased Positively (what to say instead)
You may not get up from the table until you're finished.	You may leave the table when you're finished eating.
You're not going anywhere until your room is clean!	You can go play with your friends after you clean your room.
I can't hear you when you whine like that.	I will help you out when you ask nicely.
If you won't talk to me respectfully, I will not listen to you.	I'm ready to listen to you when you use a respectful tone of voice.
Stay right there until your homework is done.	As soon as you finish your homework, you can go play.
I'm counting to three. If you're not in bed, I won't tuck you in.	I can tuck you in if you get into bed by the time I say three. One…

Same message, gentler wording.

How to Use Reinforcement

Reinforcement—both positive and negative—is most effective when it is (1) immediate, (2) realistic, (3), valuable and meaningful, (4) safe and healthy, and (5) appropriate for the context. Let's look at the descriptions and some examples of effective and ineffective reinforcers in all of these categories.

Immediate: An instantaneous response is often most effective because it strengthens the connection between the action and the reinforcer.

Effective: "I love how you're working so diligently on your math homework! I know it's not easy for you."

Ineffective: "I meant to tell you earlier—nice job on doing your homework!" (Note: this is far less effective than immediate reinforcement, but still better than no reinforcement at all.)

Realistic: The reinforcer must be something that you can and will be able to give (or, for negative reinforcement, something that you will be able to withhold). Additionally, the terms must be something your child can realistically achieve.

Effective: "If you miss the bus, I won't be able to drive you and you'll need to find another way to get to school."

Ineffective: "If you don't get yourself to school on time today, you won't be able to come on our planned vacation this weekend."

Valuable and meaningful: Learn what means the most to your child; it may be quality time over a physical prize, or an action rather than an object (and preferably not something that he gets frequently anyway or is able to buy for himself).

Effective: rewarding the highly sociable child with a later curfew

Ineffective: rewarding your child with a small sum of money after he earned a significant amount at his summer job

Safe and healthy: It must be something that's in line with your family's health and safety practices.

Effective: playing a special game together for fifteen minutes before bedtime on a school night

Ineffective: letting your child stay up past her bedtime on a school night when she does not function well without adequate sleep

Appropriate for the context: Be mindful of where, when, and how much you reinforce (don't overdo it!).

Effective: a backslap or fist bump in public, hugs in the privacy of your home

Ineffective: hugs and effusive praise in front of your tween's friends (a surefire recipe for mortifying your child)

And, as always, be sure to monitor the effectiveness of any reinforcer. Remember your mindfulness!

When to Reinforce

You can definitely plan your positive reinforcement in advance. At the same time, don't discount the value of spontaneous reinforcement. Try to catch your child behaving well as often as possible and be sure to compliment, reward, or high five him as appropriate to keep those behaviors coming. (Can't think of a good reinforcer on the spot? Say, "I want to think of a great reward for that behavior! Let's come up with some ideas and we'll discuss it later.")

Of course, you don't have to (and won't be able to) plan for every instance. Remember, negative reinforcement is often the most effective on-the-spot tactic, as long as you follow the guidelines. While you can't know what your child will do, you *can* have some effective reinforcers prepared for when you need them.

That bit of preparation can help you focus and stay calm in the heat of the moment. You've probably noticed that parenting in an emotional state of mind is rarely effective. If you're upset or agitated, your reinforcement attempts are more likely to be unproductive ("If you don't share that toy with your sister, I'm taking it away and you'll never see it again"), but if you have some reinforcers ready, you're more likely to be effective ("If you don't give your sister a turn, I'll take away the game for the rest of the evening").

We also want to consider what type of reinforcement "schedule" is most effective for the situation. We use reinforcement on two schedules: continuous and intermittent.

Continuous reinforcement is predictable, prearranged, and established. It's used to encourage behaviors that happen often—like daily teeth brushing—and is especially important when establishing and shaping a new behavior. It's also best for increasing behaviors that you want to occur more frequently.

Continuous reinforcement works like this: it attaches a desirable outcome for performing the behavior every time (*brush my teeth = get a sticker on a chart*). You must be consistent with your reward until the behavior becomes a habit. If you reinforce inconsistently or stop altogether, you may find that your child starts to lag or stops altogether too.

Once the desired behavior is firmly established, you can cut down on the frequency of the reinforcer (*get a sticker once a week and a bigger reward every six stickers*) and eventually segue into intermittent reinforcement.

Intermittent reinforcement is reinforcement that occurs at unpredictable intervals. It's like gambling: sometimes you win, sometimes you don't, but that "sometimes" is often alluring enough to make you keep trying because *maybe this time you'll hit the jackpot.*

This type of reinforcement—occasionally or spontaneously rewarding a behavior—will encourage your child to keep trying to get that feedback or reward. It makes the behavior practically indestructible, for better or for worse, so use it with caution. Giving your child a special prize in response to a random behavior will motivate him to do it again. On the flip side, giving in to a tantrum once in a while will motivate him to tantrum again (and possibly longer or louder) next time—and the time after that, and after that...

Intermittent reinforcement is effective for maintaining a behavior. Once your child has a new behavior down pat and you're ready to taper off the rewards, throw in a compliment or reward on occasion to encourage him to continue that behavior.

You'll probably encounter a lot of opportunities for intermittent reinforcement: catching your child doing his homework quietly, making a request in an appropriate tone of voice, asking for help rather than blowing up when a sibling is annoying him. The opportunity may even present itself if your child asks for a toy or other reward. You can specifically tell him, "I'm glad to take you to the ball game because you've been working really hard lately to calm down when you get upset."

Remember the teeth-brushing chart? Once your kid is brushing his teeth without complaining and you've ditched the chart (because it's finally become that well-worn path!), you can surprise him with a bonus tooth-brushing sticker or treat—or even just a compliment—every so often. That will remind him that brushing his teeth will occasionally result in a reward.

Positive Reinforcement Strategies

Now that you've learned the hows and whens of reinforcement, it's time to focus on incorporating positive reinforcement into your parenting. This is a powerful tool, and you want to harness its power effectively. One of the simplest reinforcement strategies is praise.

Praise

Praising your child is a great way to foster a healthy relationship and increase self-esteem (so it's an acceptance technique), and it's also a great reinforcer (so it's a change strategy too). It's an easy-to-use, free-of-charge, feel-good reward that's meaningful to everyone involved—when done properly.

Praise is an art. Here's how to get it right:

- **Be specific.** Avoid pat phrases like "Good job" or "You're a great kid" and replace them with "I appreciate how you listened right away" or "You put that down in just the right spot." Focus on making the praise specific to the behavior you're trying to reinforce.

- **Be genuine.** Your child can smell fake, forced praise from a mile away, and that's ineffective. (At the same time, if praising your child in these ways feel unnatural at first, like with opposite action, you can fake it till you make it, but just be sure to really mean it!)

- **Don't exaggerate.** Overdoing it takes away from the genuineness.

- **Diversify your language.** Don't always use "good" or "great" or "nice"; mix it up with "awesome" or "creative" or "beautiful" or "I love that!" If your child doesn't respond to typical praise, try showing interest by asking questions: "Can you show me how you made that?"

- **Publicize it.** Not in a way that will embarrass your child. Depending on your family situation, try to have both parents present for praise or share it with your spouse or partner when she comes home. You may also find it effective to share with others—grandparents, teachers, friends—as long as your child doesn't respond negatively to it. (She may squirm but be pleased inside!)

- **With loving touch.** Enhance the connection by delivering your praise with a hug, a kiss, a backslap, a high five, or any other affectionate gesture.

Having a hard time with praise? Remember your *cope ahead* skill and have some praise phrases ready to go. You can even practice them in front of the mirror (don't worry, nobody's watching) until you get over that awkwardness and it feels more natural.

Try these phrases:

- "I love how patient you're being! I know that you're really hungry and dinner's not ready yet, and you're waiting without a fuss."

- "I just saw you walk away from your sister when she was teasing you. That takes a lot of self-control and I'm so impressed! Gimme five!"

- "You know, in the past you'd swear and yell when I would say no to taking the car. I'm amazed that you went to your room to chill out with some music! Remind me to tell your dad about this."

- "You guys are building the coolest city and you're cooperating so nicely! Let me take a picture of it and send it to Grandma so she can see it too."

While praise is important, it's often not enough to do the trick on its own. Another effective positive reinforcement strategy is the use of behavioral charts or contracts.

Behavioral Charts and Contracts

Behavioral charts and contracts are a popular behavior-shaping strategy that can be used for children of all ages (when made developmentally appropriate for the child's age).

You may know these charts better as "sticker charts," "reward charts," "contingency contracts," or something similar. Put simply, a behavioral chart is an agreement between the parent and child: if you do this behavior, you'll get this reward. (It's not quite as dog-training-esque as it sounds, but it has a similar effect.)

The goal of behavioral charts and contracts is to target a specific behavior and increase its frequency. They can be used for simple behaviors (like staying in bed after being tucked in) or more significant behaviors (like staying calm when upset). The parent and child create an agreement with specific terms and clear expectations of what needs to happen in order to get a specified reward. You then put the terms of the agreement into writing (in a clear chart format or contract) to make it easier to see and track progress. (You'll learn how to do this, step by step, soon.)

Now, keep in mind that every behavior has an opposite behavior: back talk versus speaking respectfully, fighting versus getting along, chewing with your mouth open versus using good table manners. When you reinforce one behavior, you override the other behavior. Put another way, increasing one behavior simultaneously decreases another. (Remember the paths in the forest? The more you walk the path, the smoother it gets.)

That's why reinforcement strategies, especially behavioral charts and contracts, are effective for introducing new behaviors as well as decreasing unwanted behaviors. If you reward your child for the behavior of "not hitting," he simultaneously practices other behaviors and coping skills to replace the hitting behavior. (He may learn those replacement behaviors naturally, or you may have to suggest some alternate behaviors.)

When you continually reinforce the desired behavior, you help your child in the long term by creating and reinforcing lasting behavioral patterns. (Punishment, while useful, does not have the built-in benefit of naturally teaching new behaviors. It's effective for stopping behavior, but not as effective for replacing those behaviors with new ones.)

Effective charting is more complex than simply awarding a sticker "for good behavior"—it requires thought, planning, and follow-through. You'd probably love a magic wand to make your child compliant and obedient—or at least make him stop punching the wall, destroying your stuff, or cursing out his siblings—overnight. And a behavioral chart may seem magical at first. It works pretty quickly, but if it's not done properly, the behaviors tend to relapse quickly as well. Behavior shaping is a process that takes time and patience (and often trial and error until you get it right).

A behavioral chart may be too juvenile for an older child or teen. In this case, you can apply the same principles to a behavioral contract: write out the terms and the rewards clearly. Skip the actual chart, but follow the same guidelines.

Here's a four-step process for creating a useful and effective behavioral chart.

Step 1: Plan

The planning stage is vital; you're planning for success, and that takes careful consideration. Don't involve your child in this step yet; you'll bring him in later. Planning involves several substeps.

First, identify your goals. Set general goals, such as "improve homework performance" and "keep your room clean."

Prioritize. Pick your battles. Identify the most crucial issue right now and work on that first. (Keep a list of the other issues that you are facing to work on later.)

Example: Homework is the biggest issue right now. I can let her messy room slide (for now).

Observe and describe the behavior you want to change. Be mindful. Pay attention to how and when the behavior manifests, the frequency and intensity (these are important) of the behavior, your responses, and your child's reactions to your responses. You'll want to keep an actual log (digital or in an old-fashioned notebook). This will help you define an exact goal and later assess the effectiveness of the chart.

Following the homework example, keep track of what happens at homework time every day for a week or two. Describe how your child responds to prompts, if she tantrums, what she says, and if, when, and how the homework eventually gets done. Note how many times she refuses to do her homework weekly and try to rate the intensity of her behavior and reactions during each incident.

Example: Monday: It took her twenty minutes to finally sit down for homework. She kept making excuses to run to her room. I had to prompt her three times and she got upset before settling down and finally doing her homework. Intensity rating: 7/10

Break down the behavior. Now that you've clearly identified and defined the target behavior, use that information to help you break down the behavior into smaller, manageable tasks or pieces. This is important because behavior-shaping strategies are best practiced in small steps. A too-large, too-ambitious goal is virtually doomed to failure from the start, but entirely achievable when broken down into smaller increments. When you break down the behavior, you increase the likelihood of continuing on the path toward the larger goal. Your child is less likely to get frustrated and give up when she sees she's making progress and being rewarded for it.

It's difficult to learn complex tasks all at once; that's why kids learn basic math before jumping into advanced calculus or quantum physics! For maximum effectiveness, start small; practice and reinforce each small behavior before moving on to the next one. This ensures that the first behavior is strong before moving on to a new or deeper level. It also allows you to taper off the reinforcements once the basic behavior is firmly rooted, shifting those reinforcements to the newer behaviors. Using the example above, that means that you won't forever be rewarding your child for simply sitting down to do homework.

Example: A challenging task, like "do your homework," can be broken down into manageable time slots or pieces: sit down for homework on time, complete your math homework, focus on homework for ten minutes (increase the time as the behavior is strengthened).

Example: A larger task, like "keeping your room clean," can be broken down into steps: put laundry in the hamper, make your bed, hang up your jacket, clear the floor before bed every night.

Example: A global issue, like noncompliance, can be broken down into parts: be home by curfew, stop using foul language, turn off your phone at the dinner table.

When breaking down the behavior, define exactly what you want to change (the target behavior). Be specific. Avoid vague qualifiers such as "behaving nicely every day." Instead, define what constitutes "behaving." Clearly define the behavior and when and how it should (or shouldn't) occur. These behaviors may be physical (hitting, damaging property, throwing objects, biting, spitting, pulling hair, slamming doors), verbal (swearing, screaming, name-calling, teasing), inappropriate (lying, stealing), or related to compliance (coming home on time, cleaning her room, doing homework, completing chores, eating at the table, going to bed on time, brushing teeth, studying).

Example: Target behavior: sitting down to do homework at your desk in your room with one prompt

Step 2: Create

Now that you're crystal clear on what you're trying to change, it's time to come up with the chart (or, for older kids, the contract) itself.

Involve your child. Don't just make up the chart and present it to her; include her in discussing the terms and rewards, if age-appropriate (for a young child, set the terms yourself). She'll feel good when she sees that you value her input. That does not mean that you have to agree to whatever reward she wants! Set limits and reserve the right to veto any suggestion.

Balance acceptance and change. You're working on change; that doesn't mean you can forget about acceptance! Use your validation skills when discussing the contract or chart with your child. Use statements like "I know how hard it is to stop yourself from screaming when you're angry" or "I want to reward you for working so hard on your math homework, even though it's not easy" or "You're really hungry and tired when you get home from school, and that's tough!"

Challenge your child just enough. Too easy and it's pointless; too hard and he'll lose motivation. If your child is getting stickers or rewards 100% of the time, it's too easy. You want your child to "pass"—to earn a sticker, point, or currency of your choosing—at least 50% of the time. (Remember, you're aiming for that balancing point!) Use the information that you observed and described in the planning phase to help you decide on effective terms.

Choose an appropriate reward. Finding the right reward to effectively incentivize your child can be tricky. The obvious go-to choices are usually treats (candies, toys, electronics), which are generally effective but may not be the best option for various reasons (health, budgetary restrictions, expensive taste, an overabundance of gadgets).

Come prepared for the reward negotiations! Have a list of possible rewards (that you're willing to give) ready to share with your child, then ask for his input and ideas. That will give him an impression of the type and size of the rewards you're willing to give (so he won't be disappointed when you offer a new stuffed animal to preempt his request for a puppy). It can be helpful to offer a "prize list" with a variety of rewards for your child to cash in his stickers or tokens rather than one specific reward.

Try these suggestions:

- Time spent with a parent (playing a game, riding bikes, going out for coffee or ice cream, running errands together)

- Time spent with a friend (a sleepover or special outing, a visit with a faraway friend, a "parent-chauffeured" night out with friends)

- Choosing a favorite dinner

- Later bedtime or curfew

- Special snack or food

- Outing

- Prizes or collectibles

- Stickers, tickets, coins, or tokens (as a standalone reward or to "save up" toward a bigger reward)

- Getting picked up from school instead of taking the bus

- Screen time

- Money

- Tickets to a sporting event or concert

- Use of the car

When choosing a reward, be mindful of several factors (in addition to the reinforcement guidelines that you learned earlier in this chapter):

- **Suitability:** The reward should be appropriate for the behavior. Smaller, easier behaviors earn smaller rewards; larger, more challenging behaviors earn larger rewards.

- **Balance:** Don't overdo it. If you overreward (like promising a trip to Disneyland for completing a month-long chart), you may unwittingly create a sense of entitlement in your child.

- **Flexibility:** You can change up the rewards (and the terms of earning them) as necessary. A reward may start to lose its appeal after it's been earned a few times or as the current fads change.

- **Current privileges:** While it's usually best to implement a new reward, sometimes kids get everything they want without actually earning it. Think about your child's regular privileges and reconsider that regularity; you may want to turn one of those privileges into an earnable reward. For example, if every child gets dessert regardless of what she or he has eaten, you may now decide that dessert is now a reward for those who finish a predetermined part of their dinner. (Expect some pushback in the beginning if your child is used to receiving that reward without any strings attached! Changing her mindset will most likely take some time.)

If you're concerned about spoiling your kids with an abundance of rewards, you're not alone. Studies have shown that overusing external rewards to motivate a child may decrease the child's natural drive to do the right thing (Kohn 1993; Pink 2009).

While the negative effects of overrewarding are certainly a valid reason for concern, a healthy balance is necessary. When rewards are used effectively and thoughtfully, they can and do help children change their behavior in the long term. We'll get into this concept in more depth at the end of the chapter, in the Roadblocks to Reinforcement section.

Draw up the chart. Once you've established the terms and conditions, it's time to make the chart itself. When age-appropriate (and personality-appropriate), have your child create the chart by hand or digitally and decorate it. He'll be more motivated if he participates in setting up the chart, and it's a great opportunity for a collaborative bonding activity.

The chart can be as simple or as elaborate as you'd like: a hand-drawn chart on construction paper, a computer-designed table, or a colorful poster. I recommend a calendar-style table with the days of the week on top and enough boxes to accommodate the number of times your child will need to perform the behavior. (You can use the information you gathered in the planning phase to help you figure out how much time your child will need.) This will serve as an at-a-glance progress tracker, enabling you to monitor your child's "success rate" easily. Read on to see samples of a completed chart and contract. You can also find templates for a basic chart and a contract at http://www.newharbinger.com/46868.

Be clear. State the terms clearly and write them down on the chart or contract (or on a separate sheet hung nearby). If you're discussing it verbally, make sure to state these terms explicitly; however, it's best to write them as well so that there's no room for debate. Explain exactly what is expected of your child:

What: getting ready for bed on time

When: by 8:00 on school nights and 9:30 on weekends

How: with one prompt or warning (earn an extra sticker for getting ready without any prompting)

Rewards: small rewards for 10 stickers; larger rewards for 40 stickers

When the terms are there in black and white, there's no room for power struggles; you're all on the same page. Be sure to review it with your child and have him repeat it back to you to make sure that he really understands it.

For a young child or struggling reader, try illustrating the chart or adding pictures of your child acting out the behavior. Motivate him by adding pictures of the prizes or encouraging phrases like "I know you can do it!" or "I believe in you!"

Suggest different behaviors or solutions to replace the target behavior. To help your child choose a different "pathway," offer him alternative ways to deal with his frustrations or problems. Having a solution will empower and enable him to pick the better "path" and help him succeed. "Instead of hitting, come tell me that your sister is teasing you." "If you need to punch something, use your bed or a punching bag." "When you're mad, go shoot some hoops in the driveway."

Sometimes, the alternative behavior can do double duty and help your child calm down. Try putting the chart in his room and sending him up to put on a sticker. Every time he gets that reinforcer, he automatically removes himself from an emotionally charged situation, which gives him space to calm down.

Step 3: Implement

You've finished laying the groundwork; now it's time to put it into action.

Go public. When appropriate (assuming it won't humiliate your child), hang the chart in a prominent place. If she's okay with it, share her accomplishments with Grandma or others in her life.

Show interest. Follow up with verbal praise and don't allow the chart to slide into oblivion once the novelty wears off! Incorporate praise whenever possible: when she earns a sticker, when she earns a prize, whenever you see her performing her new behavior. Even kids who aren't usually receptive of praise often accept it when it comes along with a reward.

Make it her responsibility. Let her mark off the accomplishments by herself for a sense of satisfaction and to keep the chart fresh in her mind. That check is a reinforcer in and of itself; she'll feel pride and accomplishment whenever she marks her progress.

You may entrust an older child with the task of keeping track of his own behavior (as long as he does not have a tendency to lie). An honor system-style contract shows him that you trust him and gives him a sense of responsibility for his own actions.

Step 4: Evaluate and Adapt

After you've put all that work into the chart or contract, you want to make sure it's working.

Monitor and observe the effectiveness consistently. Check in with your child (and your partner), review the chart on a regular basis to evaluate its effectiveness, and adjust when necessary. Compare the behavior to the baseline that you observed in the planning phase. Be mindful! This is an ongoing process, not a set-it-and-forget-it activity.

Modify the terms. Remember how you broke down the goal into smaller goals? Once you've established that first smaller goal and the behavior is solid, you can change the terms and start working on the next step toward your long-term goal.

Move forward. When you've accomplished the long-term goal (woohoo!), extend the periods of time between rewards and then taper off the rewards, doling out larger rewards (so he doesn't protest against the unfairness of it all) at less frequent intervals. Once you stop the rewards entirely, be sure to intermittently reinforce the desired behavior on occasion to keep it strong!

Reinforcement in Action

Let's see how some parents try out these skills in the following scenarios.

Scenario #1: The Combative Kid

Life with eight-year-old Julian is tough, especially for his siblings. Whenever he's upset about anything (which seems to be all the time), he takes it out on them: pushing, hitting, pulling their hair, scratching…and that's just the physical aggression. He also teases them to the point of tears. From the moment he comes home, Mom's counting down the hours until bedtime.

(Sound familiar?)

At her wit's end, Mom decides to make up a chart for Julian. She prints out a blank calendar page and buys a sheet of Star Wars stickers (Julian's favorites). She sits him down and informs him that this is his "no-fighting chart." She writes down the rules in simple language: for every day that he doesn't fight, he gets a sticker. If he gets a sticker every day this week, at the end of the week he'll get that new R2-D2 figurine he's been hankering after.

Mom posts the chart on the fridge, and everyone's excited—especially when Julian proudly sticks his first sticker on and everyone goes to bed happily.

It lasts two days.

On day three, Julian whacks his brother for touching his light saber without permission. No sticker for Julian. And for the rest of the week, the fighting's back in full force.

Where did Mom go wrong?

1. Mom takes over the entire chart process; Julian is not involved at all.

2. Mom's goal is unrealistic and too big for Julian; it may be too difficult for him to switch from constantly fighting to not fighting for the entire day.

3. The behavior—"no fighting"—is vague and includes too many behaviors at once (both physical and verbal fighting).

4. Mom takes an all-or-nothing approach: Julian needs a sticker every day in order to get the reward. Once he loses that chance, he has no motivation to continue.

5. There are no long-term goals planned; Julian would get a valuable (to him) prize after a short time, decreasing his motivation once he gets his coveted R2-D2. Once he earns that—after just one week of not fighting—what's next? Another figurine every week will lose its value pretty quickly, and it can be overwhelming to create a new chart every week. A long-term chart will help him establish long-lasting behaviors and smooth out that path in his brain.

Let's give Mom some recognition and positive reinforcement for the things that she *does* do right: she chooses a valuable reward, writes down the rules, and rewards Julian immediately at the end of the day. Go Mom!

So what would be more effective?

Mom invites Dad and Julian to a "family meeting." She tells them that she's noticed a problem with fighting every day and that she'd like the house to be a calmer, safer place for everyone. She tells Julian that she would like to create a chart for him, mentioning that it can be really hard to control oneself after a long day of school: "I know how hard this is for you, and I want to reward you for trying so hard!"

Together, they identify the worst times of the day (right after school and on weekend mornings). They decide to address those times for now. Mom tells Julian that she knows he really wants that R2-D2 and asks if that's what he'd like to earn, and he excitedly agrees.

With input from Julian and Dad, Mom makes up the chart on the computer (with Julian advising her on the layout and decorations), listing the terms clearly:

Who: Julian

What: no physical fighting (hitting, spitting, pulling hair, pushing)

When: school days from 3:30 to 5:30 p.m. and weekends from 8:30 to 10:30 a.m.

Prizes earned: a sticker for every two-hour period. Julian can earn small rewards for 3 stickers (a donut, a Slurpee, a game with Mom or Dad, 5 minutes of extra screen time) and larger rewards for 15 stickers (R2-D2 figurine, a trip to the ice cream store, a new game app)

What's next? After the first cycle, we'll start over, with one change: the time period will now be 3 hours instead of 2. Possible prizes: a Star Wars LEGO set or a Darth Vader mask (Mom and Julian will make up a wish list together)

Julian's Chart

Sunday	Monday	Tuesday	Wednesday	Thursday	Friday	Saturday
8:30-10:30 AM ☐	3:30-5:30 PM ☐	3:30-5:30 PM ☐	3:30-5:30 PM ☐	3:30-5:30 PM ☐	3:30-5:30 PM ☐	8:30-10:30 AM ☐
8:30-10:30 AM ☐	3:30-5:30 PM ☐	3:30-5:30 PM ☐	3:30-5:30 PM ☐	3:30-5:30 PM ☐	3:30-5:30 PM ☐	8:30-10:30 AM ☐
8:30-10:30 AM ☐	3:30-5:30 PM ☐	3:30-5:30 PM ☐	3:30-5:30 PM ☐	3:30-5:30 PM ☐	3:30-5:30 PM ☐	8:30-10:30 AM ☐
8:30-10:30 AM ☐	3:30-5:30 PM ☐	3:30-5:30 PM ☐	3:30-5:30 PM ☐	3:30-5:30 PM ☐	3:30-5:30 PM ☐	8:30-10:30 AM ☐

How to earn checks/stickers: every two-hour period without fighting

Small Prizes
(3 stickers):
Donut
Slurpee
Game with Mom or Dad
15 minutes extra screen time

Large Prizes
(15 stickers):
R2-D2 figurine
Trip to ice cream store
New game app

I CAN DO IT! GO JULIAN!

They print it out, stick it on the fridge with a sheet of stickers attached, and get to work.

This chart sets Julian up for success. Why?

1. He's involved, which makes him feel important and heard.

2. Long- and short-term goals are in place and broken down into small, manageable pieces before starting.

3. The terms are specific and realistic.

4. The prizes are appropriate for the difficulty of the work Julian has to do.

5. If Julian messes up one day, he can start fresh the next day.

Will Julian mess up? Sure. And that's normal! (If he doesn't mess up, that means that the goal is too easy.) But this chart is much more likely to result in a calmer, happier home for Julian and the entire family.

Plus, let's be realistic. Even if Mom does everything "right," sometimes it doesn't work out. And that's okay, too—no judgment! That's when she'd go back to the drawing board and examine what went wrong: Are the expectations too high? Does he have the skills to regulate his emotions? Does he need more immediate rewards? Should she try a different strategy entirely? Remember dialectics: nothing will work for everyone all the time.

The evaluate and adapt phase is crucial for success: it helps Mom and Julian stay on track (and also demonstrates flexibility on Mom's part, for bonus points!).

Scenario #2: The Mouthy Teen

Thirteen-year-old Ellie has never been the easiest kid (and that's putting it mildly), but the start of adolescence has catapulted her into an entirely new category. She's become extremely disrespectful and explosive, mouthing off at her parents at (seemingly) every opportunity. She's verbally aggressive, uses inappropriate language, and tends to aim most of her painful barbs at Mom, especially when she's unhappy with whatever Mom has made for dinner (and being a picky eater, that happens frequently).

Typical punishments have not helped; as a matter of fact, they've made things worse.

Mom has resorted to banning Ellie from the table for the entire dinnertime, which has only resulted in hours-long tirades and Ellie raiding the fridge and pantry once everyone has gone to sleep.

She decides to try her hand at positive reinforcement and offers Ellie an incentive: For each day she speaks respectfully to Mom, she'll get an extra two dollars of allowance.

Ellie's thrilled about that—up to fourteen dollars extra a week! She immediately reins herself in, being careful to speak respectfully, and quickly racks up some extra cash. Even when she misses a day, which happens rather frequently (like when Mom made meatloaf and she screamed, "Don't you know that I ****ing hate meatloaf? You're such an idiot; it tastes like %$@#!"), but she continues to get money at least a few times a week.

Somehow, Mom finds herself with rapidly emptying pockets and a daughter who still attacks her verbally on a regular basis.

What went wrong?

1. Mom doesn't focus on a specific goal or break down her goal into small steps.

2. Mom doesn't involve Ellie in the planning stage.

3. Because the goal is targeting a too-vague, too-large behavior, Ellie is able to earn rewards without making too much effort; she's rewarded even on days when it's easy for her to keep her cool.

How can Mom effectively clean up Ellie's language?

At a calm time, Mom sits Ellie down for a chat. She starts off with validation: "Ellie, I know it really bothers you when you get home from school and you don't like what's for dinner. I get it! You've had a long day and you're tired and starving, and it's disappointing and frustrating to find out that dinner is something you don't like. Your language is really affecting the atmosphere in our house, and it's really hurtful sometimes. I'd like to help you express yourself more appropriately. Can we work on a plan together to make this work for all of us?"

They decide to start by targeting the days on which Ellie doesn't like dinner. Mom proposes a few alternative phrases that Ellie can use instead of insults and swearing and asks Ellie to offer a few of her own. She also asks Ellie to come up with a list of things that she'd like to earn, stipulating that she (Mom) has ultimate veto power.

Some of Ellie's suggestions are nixed (like a skydiving trip and purple highlights) or tweaked (like choosing the dinner menu for the week). Together, they decide on a list of long-term rewards: new bed sheets, a new bag (up to a specified value), a day off of school, and a trip to visit a faraway friend. The short-term reward list includes a smoothie from the ice cream store, choosing the dinner menu for a night, a set of bath bombs, and a five dollar bonus on her allowance.

Mom and Ellie draw up an informal contract, stating the terms and conditions:

- When Ellie does not like dinner, she will express herself in a calm tone of voice and with respectful language: no swearing, no yelling, no name-calling. She may have one prompt from Mom or Dad, which gives her one chance to start over if she forgets.

- Ellie may choose to make her own dinner: cereal, yogurt, toaster waffles, or a sandwich.

- For every four checks that Ellie earns for speaking respectfully, she may choose a reward from the smaller-reward list.

- After eighteen checks, Ellie earns a larger reward.

My Contract

Name: ELLIE

Date: 6/15/2020

Specific behavior I'm trying to change: VERBAL AGGRESSION (SWEARING, YELLING, NAME-CALLING) WHEN I'M UNHAPPY ABOUT DINNER

Terms & conditions in order to earn rewards: WHEN I DON'T LIKE DINNER, I WILL EXPRESS MYSELF IN A CALM TONE OF VOICE AND WITH RESPECTFUL LANGUAGE. I HAVE ONE CHANCE TO START OVER IF I FORGET (WITH A PROMPT FROM MOM OR DAD). INSTEAD OF DINNER, I MAY EAT CEREAL, YOGURT, TOASTER WAFFLES, OR A SANDWICH

Rewards List

Reward	Value	Reward	Value
SMOOTHIE	4 CHECKS	NEW BEDSHEETS	18 CHECKS
CHOOSE DINNER	4 CHECKS	NEW BAG	18 CHECKS
BATH BOMBS	4 CHECKS	DAY OFF FROM SCHOOL	18 CHECKS
$5 ALLOWANCE BONUS	4 CHECKS	VISIT TO JULIA	18 CHECKS

Child's signature: ELLIE

Parent's signature: *Mom*

Suddenly, dinnertime is a lot more pleasant in Ellie's house.

After the second small reward, Mom mentions to Ellie that she's noticed how much the atmosphere has improved, and she offers Ellie an opportunity to earn her larger rewards sooner: she can also earn an extra check by speaking respectfully when she's frustrated about homework (another target area).

This system works better for Ellie because

1. Mom shows Ellie that she values her opinions and feelings and they collaborate on a contract (and Ellie thinks of rewards that Mom would not have considered);

2. the target behavior is very specific, and the short- and long-term goals are defined;

3. Ellie only earns rewards when she deserves them; and

4. Mom evaluates the plan constantly and introduces new behaviors when Ellie is ready for them.

Roadblocks to Reinforcement

The road to behavior change may be blocked by various factors that interfere with your effectiveness. The most common roadblocks to using reinforcement effectively, or at all, are shown below. You can also download the Chapter 6 Roadblock Cards at http://www.newharbinger.com/46868.

Roadblock (the statement)	Detour (the solution)
He shouldn't be hitting in the first place, so why am I rewarding him for NOT hitting?	Abandon "should"—focus on what is and what works.
She knows what's right and what's wrong!	"Right" is learned—it's not inborn and must be taught. Additionally, knowing doesn't always translate into doing; she may not have the skills to act appropriately, or she may have been reinforced to act this way, forming a habit.

Roadblock (the statement)	Detour (the solution)
He's only behaving this way to get a reinforcer. It's manipulative! *She's just looking for attention!* *He's not really scared to go to school; he just wants to avoid the situation.*	Children often don't know what's subconsciously driving their behavior. Even if she's just looking for attention, she may not be doing it on purpose! Use your mindful Describe skill without judgment.
I don't have the time or patience for this.	Yes, reinforcement takes time and effort. But if you examine all of the time and effort expended on dealing with your child's behavior, you may find that reinforcement is equally or less time-consuming and difficult! (Try it out, with just one child and just one behavior, and see what happens.)
Why should I bribe my child to behave?	Bribery is a short-term solution—it's persuading your child to do what you want *right now*. Reinforcement is a long-term solution; it teaches an alternative behavior (and it also helps in the short term!).
He'll revert to the old behavior as soon as he stops getting the reward.	Reinforcement—when done properly and tapered off effectively—will teach your child long-lasting strategies and create new behavior "pathways."
If she gets rewarded for everything she does, she'll expect rewards for everything for the rest of her life! The real world doesn't work this way.	Reinforcement helps rewire your child's brain and behavior patterns, helping her learn to condition herself. Eventually, she can learn to reward herself to improve her own behavior in "the real world."

As noted earlier, one roadblock that gets in the way of reinforcement for many parents is the idea that extrinsic (i.e., external) rewards have a significant harmful effect on a child's ability to motivate himself. Some profess that this effect can have lifelong consequences. A significant body of research, spanning decades, decries the use of rewards (Deci and Ryan 1985; Lepper, Greene, and Nisbett 1973; Gagné and Deci 2005; Eisenberger, Pierce, and Cameron 1999; Frey and Jegen 2000). These studies suggest that linking behavior with rewards leads to diminished self-motivation and drive.

However, research has also shown that incentive plans, when implemented properly, can and do work to shape behavior (Ledford, Gerhart, and Fang 2013; Cameron and Pierce 1994). First, the negative effects of external rewards do not apply to intermittent reinforcement. When rewards are unpredictable, rather than expected, they do not diminish internal motivation. Additionally, verbal rewards (AKA praise) have been shown to significantly increase intrinsic, or internal, motivation. That's why it's so important to include praise in your reward systems!

When executed properly, external rewards do not necessarily inhibit intrinsic motivation. We use extrinsic motivation to help children tap into their not-yet-accessed intrinsic motivation. It can be difficult for kids to naturally motivate themselves, so we attach external rewards to help them along. If we include plenty of praise and observe the effects of their improved behavior, we effectively use extrinsic rewards to access their intrinsic motivation.

When you set up a behavioral chart for your child, praise him when he earns a sticker, a token, and a reward. Tell him how proud you are of him for working so hard. Point out how he's getting into fewer fights with you and with his siblings and how the house is so much more peaceful and fun. The rewards will eventually be phased out, but the lessons that he learns as he earns them will last.

In short, like everything in life, the right balance is key. Rewards are a valuable addition to a parent's skill toolbox, and when they're utilized correctly, they will enhance intrinsic motivation.

You've learned why it's important to reinforce your child's behavior; it's just as important to reinforce yourself! You may notice that your children's behavior is negatively reinforcing your own behavior. When your kids start to bicker, you'll do what you can to make it stop (and to avoid the swift descent into full-blown mayhem). Eventually you'll figure out the triggers and recognize the signs of an imminent fight, then break it up before it escalates. For example, you may find that the biggest fights start when your kids are bored, so you suggest a game when you notice them getting edgy. You're buckling your seatbelt before the beeping starts!

In those moments, when a fight is brewing and you just want it to stop, you may use certain parenting strategies (whether they're "good" or not) because they seem to work. The one that works for you—without fail—is screaming at them. So you do it again. And again. Even though it upsets everyone (including you), you keep screaming at them because it works.

And it's really hard to change your behavior once it's reinforced over and over again!

Screaming might be effective in the short term, but it definitely has negative consequences: on your children, on your self-respect, and on your parent-child relationship. If you really want to change that behavior, have a frank talk with yourself and think about a different strategy that you can use to get similar results.

Praise yourself when you choose an effective strategy instead of resorting to yelling. Give yourself a check on your mental (or even physical!) chart every time you do it, and reward yourself appropriately when you act effectively.

You can even use reinforcement on yourself for reinforcing your kids! Commit to praising your kids once a day. Set a reminder on your phone if you need to. When that becomes more habitual, increase your goal to twice a day per child, slowly increasing the goals as you progress. And don't forget those rewards! Go out for coffee with a friend, buy yourself that sinful chocolate and hide it from the kids, or put away money toward something you really want for yourself.

Reinforcement is an important tool in your parenting toolbox for gently shaping your child's behavior. While reinforcement is highly effective for encouraging change and building behaviors, an additional set of strategies, which you'll learn in the next chapter, is designed to decrease your child's less-than-desirable behaviors.

CHAPTER 7

Change Strategies to Reduce Unwanted Behavior

Everyone knows one unfailingly positive parent: the super-smiley mom; the my-child-can-do-no-wrong dad; the optimistic, upbeat, we-only-use-affirmative-language-in-our-house couple. And while that parent most likely gets under your skin, you've probably found yourself wishing that *you* could always be that positive.

Guess what? Positivity isn't always the answer in parenthood.

The reality is that not all behaviors can be effectively shaped using reinforcement and other positive behavior-shaping strategies. Whereas the techniques presented in chapter 6 are used to *increase wanted behavior*, the strategies in this chapter are designed to *reduce unhelpful, unwanted behaviors*.

Don't be scared off by words like "discipline," "punishment," or "consequences" when it comes to stopping unwanted behaviors. In a world where positivity is overemphasized, especially in parenting, you may feel hesitant to actively discourage your child's behavior. But behavior-change strategies are vital components of effective parenting *and* can and do coexist peacefully with acceptance and affirmation.

Yes, positivity is crucial; that's why we start with acceptance and gentler strategies. The strategies in this chapter are just as important as the positive strategies, though they are recommended for use in smaller doses. Think of these techniques as the salt in your parenting recipe: you'll need them to complement and bring out the other flavors, but too much will ruin your dish.

In this chapter, you'll learn:

- Strategies to reduce unwanted behavior

- How to use punishment (AKA consequences) effectively

- How and when to use extinction and satiation techniques

- How to overcome obstacles to punishment, extinction, and satiation

Punishment

Punishment tends to get a bad rap in parenting today. It brings to mind harsh reprimands ("Go stand in the corner; you're punished!"), spankings, and scary authority figures.

Many parents struggle with punishment. This may be because they've had negative experiences with people (their own parents, a boss, a toxic friend) who are punitive, controlling, or abusive. Punishment by the hands of these people is generally extreme and delivered in an emotional state, which makes it ineffective and damaging. Parents who were overpunished as children may swing to the opposite extreme, overcompensate, and become overly permissive.

As a result, the word "punishment" has become nearly taboo in modern parenting (*you should* never *punish your children; it's cruel!*). Your unofficial neighborhood parenting guru and those super-positive mommy bloggers warn against the evils of punishment, suggesting that parents turn to "consequences" instead.

The difference between "punishment" and "consequences," however, is largely a matter of semantics.

Many parents define "punishment" as that archaic and unnecessarily harsh method that only taught them to fear their own parents. They define "consequences" as something that happens as a result of the behavior. In this book, we will define punishment as the act of attaching a consequence to a behavior in order to decrease and weaken the behavior.

Ineffective punishment is the kind that we've learned to fear: harsh, emotional, aggressive, scary, and shame inducing, a method for exerting control over a child.

Effective punishment is interchangeable with the gentler term "consequences," which many parents prefer. Effective punishment is used to modify the behavior, help the child learn to take responsibility for his actions, and teach the child new behavior. It is linked to the behavior and is not completely driven by emotion.

Done properly, punishment plays an important role in parenting and can be quite effective in the long run. When it's used effectively and mindfully, punishment will not negatively affect your child or your relationship with him.

Just as reinforcement has positive and negative types, there are also positive and negative punishment approaches. The same definitions apply:

Positive = adding something

Negative = removing or avoiding something

Positive punishment is the act of adding an unwanted consequence in order to stop the behavior. Examples of positive punishment include:

- Time-out

- Extra chores

- Paying for damages

- Early bedtime

- Reprimands, scolding, yelling

Some notes about time-out: Removing a child from the situation is often effective, especially for toddlers and young children. It serves as a consequence and also gives the child (and other children) the space and time to calm down. A good rule of thumb for time-out is one minute per year of age (e.g., the seven-year-old gets seven minutes).

Time-out should take place in a quiet, safe space: on the steps, in the child's room, in a quiet room. It is significantly less effective to have a "time-out" among other people or in a stimulating environment. Also avoid sending your child to the corner or any small space, which can feel more punitive.

Time-out should only start once the child is calm and quiet. She needs that quiet time to experience and process the consequence—that's the point of time-out! If you end the time-out when she's still screaming, crying, or talking to you, she may think that her screaming or bargaining caused the time-out to end. That behavior is then reinforced, and the time-out doesn't accomplish its purpose.

You may have noticed that corporal punishment—hitting or other forms of physical punishment—isn't on the list. I strongly recommend against hitting, in part because it is almost always a result of high emotion or anger. More importantly, physical punishment potentially can—and often does—result in long-term emotional and physical harm. Even in the short term, studies have shown that children who are spanked are far more likely to solve their own problems with physical violence (Simons and Wurtele 2010).

I personally do not use this strategy with my own children, and I have seen countless parents succeed in parenting without resorting to physical punishment. Research has shown that the vast majority of parents in the United States have used corporal punishment at some point (Gershoff et al. 2012), but there are so many lower-risk, highly effective strategies to use.

Let's move on to *negative punishment*, which means removing something that your child wants in order to stop or prevent the behavior. Examples include:

- Grounding

- Loss of privileges

- Loss of allowance

- Taking away a toy

- Loss of an outing or activity

One benefit of negative punishment is that you don't need to come up with a consequence to impose. Instead, you can take stock of your child's current privileges and see what can be taken away as an effective punishment.

Pros and Cons of Punishment

There's a reason we use punishment. It works! One advantage of effective punishment is that it puts a stop to the behavior. Introducing a strongly aversive consequence can stop the problem behavior in the moment, so it is most effective when your child is engaged in very problematic behavior. It gives your child the strong, clear message that her behavior is not okay and that she cannot continue to act that way without a consequence. These behaviors may include physical aggression, property destruction, coming home much later than curfew, stealing, or openly defying your instructions.

Another advantage of punishment is that it gives a strong message to your child that his behavior is simply not okay. (In contrast, avoiding punishment gives the message that his behavior is okay, which you don't want to do.)

Finally, punishment helps your child develop self-control. Permissive parenting, in which many unacceptable behaviors are overlooked ("Just ignore it and he'll stop!"), tends to be a highly ineffective parenting style. A survey of 1,141 primary caregivers of young children found that the children most at risk of low self-regulation (in other words, difficulty controlling their cognition, emotions, and behavior) were those who had parents with permissive parenting styles. Data showed that children of parents who "avoid punishing their child" or "do not confront their children regarding their behavior" tended to have weaker self-regulation skills (Piotrowski, Lapierre, and Linebarger 2013).

A lack of *appropriate* punishment impacts children's long-term ability to control their own emotions and behavior. If they do not learn to see the consequences of their actions, they'll be unable—and unwilling—to take responsibility for their behavior or control their impulses. This trait will likely follow them into adulthood.

So if punishment is a valuable technique, why not use it all the time? You've likely punished your child plenty of times; it's probably worked.

While it's a key part of parenting, punishment also has several disadvantages. First of all, it's not a feel-good strategy. As with other areas of parenting, balance is key in using consequences. Just like negative reinforcement, punishment will likely make your child feel uncomfortable. That feeling generally leads to change, but be aware that overuse may cause your child to engage in self-punishment, consciously or subconsciously. Punishment can lead to thoughts like *I get punished all the time, I must be bad, I'm a failure,* and *I can't do anything right.* This can have lasting harmful effects on a child's self-worth and self-image.

Too much punishment can also significantly damage the parent-child relationship. It may result in a child feeling that his parents don't love him or don't see any good in him.

Another disadvantage of punishment is that, while it's often effective in the short term, it tends to be the least effective for long-term behavior change. That's because it often stops the behavior in the moment but doesn't teach new behavior for the long term. The poor behaviors won't disappear on their own.

Have you ever wondered why ex-convicts often commit crimes again after serving jail time? You'd think that the punishment would be a strong enough deterrent, but there are many repeat offenders. The average prison sentence doesn't meet the guidelines for effective punishment: it's not closely related to the behavior, it doesn't happen immediately after the offense (there's usually a lengthy court process), and it doesn't teach or reinforce a preferable behavior. This last factor is a common complaint about the justice system: inmates receive no therapy, no support in reentering society, and no guidance to help them make better choices.

When you take a toy away from your child after she bops her brother over the head with it, that consequence effectively stops the behavior (and may make her think twice before she does it again). However, it doesn't teach or reinforce a different behavior that she can use the next time her brother tries to grab her toy. Sometimes the immediate disapproval ("You hurt your brother; that's not okay!") and the ensuing consequence ("Now you can't play with that toy until tomorrow") is enough to discourage her from repeating the behavior. However, that usually only happens when the child already knows a replacement behavior.

A final downside of punishment is that it can cause your child to suppress or hide the behavior in the presence of the punisher (that's you!) out of fear of punishment. That doesn't mean that he'll stop doing it; he'll just stop doing it *when you're around.*

Now, we *do* want our children to suppress their behavior; that's the whole point of punishment. We *don't* want them to learn to hide that behavior from you and continue doing it. They need to learn or strengthen a different behavior to replace the negative behavior. We suppress the behavior to stop them from doing it *while* we reinforce more appropriate behavior and empower them to make better choices. (You'll learn how to do that later in this chapter.)

The How-Tos of Effective Punishment

While punishment can be necessary at times, it should be used sparingly and with discretion.

As always, effectiveness is the name of the game. Evaluate your consequences to see if they're working; if not, stop using them. (*Sending him to his room gets him out of my hair, but he still talks back to me. Time to try a new tactic!*)

Effectiveness is closely tied to the parent's own attitude, body language, tone, and emotion. If you approach punishment as a method for stopping behavior and teaching new behavior, it will likely be effective; if you approach it as a mode of control and power over your child, it's likely to fail. Be mindful of your actions and feelings to ensure that your punishments fit the "effective" criteria instead of crossing the line to punitive, old-school, ineffective punishment.

Effective punishment fits these criteria:

Specific: Make the terms of the punishment clear to your child (and yourself) so that it doesn't lead to further power struggles or negotiation.

> *Effective:* "You lost ten minutes of playtime tomorrow because you didn't come back on time."

> *Ineffective:* "You're going to have to come in earlier next time because you didn't come back on time."

Time-limited: Don't mete out a vague, unending punishment.

> *Effective:* "I will not take you out shopping this weekend like we planned because you took twenty dollars from my purse."

Ineffective: "You are grounded until you learn how to control yourself."

Meaningful: The consequence should affect your child in a real way.

Effective: "You hit your sister with your ball. I'm taking it away until Sunday."

Ineffective: "You will spend the next two afternoons in your room" (which happens to be loaded with toys and video games).

Appropriate: Be sure the severity of the consequence fits the "crime"; a small infraction shouldn't incur a large punishment, and vice versa.

Effective: "Sneaking out of your room after curfew means you're grounded for one week."

Ineffective: "You came home ten minutes late today, so you can't play outside for the next two days."

Closely related to the behavior: The terms of the punishment should logically fit the "offense" so that your child makes a connection between her behavior and the consequences. Ask yourself: *What do I want her to learn from this consequence?*

Effective: "The money to fix the wall that you damaged has to come out of your savings."

Ineffective: "You threw that toy at the window; now you lost your allowance."

Finite: After the punishment period ends, immediately remove or stop the punishing conditions and start fresh. Move on; don't keep bringing it up or holding it over your child.

Effective: "Here's your allowance for this week. I'm glad you earned it back, and I hope we won't have to take it away again. What are you going to buy with it?"

Ineffective: "Okay, so *this* week you didn't lose your allowance, but don't think I forgot about what happened last week."

As I pointed out earlier, consequences in and of themselves do not teach your child a replacement behavior. She may genuinely not know any better way to deal with the situation at hand, or she may need help strengthening a new behavior. In order to be as effective as possible, be sure that your child knows an alternative behavior that she can use in similar situations: "If your friend is teasing you, tell the teacher or another adult instead of punching him." "When you're angry, here are some things to try: take some time to calm down in your room, take a walk, breathe deeply, or listen to music." "If you're not happy about what I made for dinner, you can ask me if there are any other options."

Consequences are most effective when used in conjunction with behavior-shaping strategies like reinforcement to teach and strengthen an alternative behavior. After the consequence, when your child is calm, take the opportunity to discuss different ways to deal with the problem. Use your chapter 6 skills here! As soon as you see her use a replacement behavior, reinforce, reinforce, reinforce—with positivity and praise.

Sometimes, replacement behaviors can be built into the punishment. When feasible, require your child to correct his behavior and go a step further: fix the effects of his behavior, and then leave the situation even better than it was. "I told you that painting in the playroom is off-limits. You need to clean the paint off of the floor and table, and while you're at it, organize the arts-and-crafts shelf in the closet."

This is known as *overcorrection*, and it tends to be more effective than simply correcting the behavior. Don't get into arguments if he protests ("No fair, I didn't mess up the closet!"); simply tell him what he has to do, and withhold something until the task is complete. "Your friends can come back when the playroom and the closet are clean."

Overcorrection is also sometimes known as "positive practice" because it requires your child to perform a positive behavior. It's more effective than punishment alone; it helps strengthen the replacement behavior. "Let's practice closing the door nicely ten times instead of slamming it." "Please say three nice things to your sister because you called her a baby." "Pick up the dirty socks and put them in your hamper, and then take them back out and do it again."

Avoid the "don'ts" of implementing consequences for ultimate effectiveness. These don'ts include:

Don't use harmful consequences. A consequence should never be related to a child's fundamental needs: food, shelter, or love. "Go to your room; no dinner for you tonight!" "Stay outside until you've learned your lesson!"

Don't demean or belittle your child. Instead, speak calmly and respectfully. Statements like "Kids your age don't act like this" or "I'll show you who's in charge here; maybe you'll think twice next time" or "Are you crazy?!" are unhelpful.

Don't be sarcastic or show disgust. That will make your child feel bad about himself, and he's likely to lash out or shut down in defense. Avoid saying things like "Oh, look who finally decided to show up an hour after curfew!" or "I can't believe a child of mine would behave like that; I'm so embarrassed. I can't even look at you."

Don't get involved in negotiations or power struggles. Give out the consequence assertively and don't get sucked in to haggling over the terms. Once you enter a power struggle, you hit a downward spiral: "Well, I don't care what you say, I don't have to pay for the stupid lamp!" "Oh, you *will* care when I take away all of your privileges!"

Don't give in to tantrums or cries of "It's not fair!" It can be easy to second-guess yourself when your child is wailing about how unfair the consequence is, but giving in will undo your hard work. (Worse, it will intermittently reinforce the behavior and she'll tantrum twice as long next time!) Stand firm; if you followed the guidelines, you can be confident in your punishment.

Don't combine punishment with existing reinforcement. Consequences should *never* be related to any reinforcement schedule that you have in place. If your child is earning stickers toward a prize, don't penalize him by removing a sticker or prize that he's already earned if he behaves badly (especially if the behavior is not related to the reinforcement).

Don't always punish immediately. Generally, it's important to punish immediately so that your child associates the consequence with the behavior. However, in some circumstances, punishing a child immediately can be ineffective. At these times, it's okay to tell your child that there will be a consequence later. Here are some situations where it's best to delay punishment.

First, when your child is out of control, punishing her right away will likely agitate her further and escalate the behavior, which can cause the situation to rapidly spiral downward. She'll be unreceptive to the consequences and will likely learn nothing from the experience. Remove her from the situation if necessary, and then calmly deal with the consequences once she's calm.

Second, factor in your own emotional state. Don't punish when you are in a state of heightened emotion. Be mindful! Handing out consequences when you're angry or frustrated is bound to be ineffective. Wait until you're calm to come up with the appropriate consequence (and deliver it in a more controlled state of mind). This also models restraint for your highly emotional child, showing him how to handle strong emotions.

Third, sometimes it's hard to think of a consequence on the spot, even if you or your child are not overly upset. If you can't come up with an effective consequence immediately, you may find yourself giving a consequence that you'll later regret. Instead, tell him that there will be a consequence and you'll let him know what it is later.

When your child acts out (especially if the behavior is not especially egregious), you can use a later opportunity to give an appropriate consequence. The consequence may even present itself! For example, your child calls you "stupid" in a heated moment. You may choose to let it slide, but when he asks you to play a game with him five minutes later, go ahead and tell him (calmly) that you are not available to play with him after he spoke to you that way.

Natural Consequences

Natural consequences, as the name implies, are consequences of your child's behavior that occur without your intervention—*naturally*. You may know them better as "learning the hard way." (As Julius Caesar said: "Experience is the teacher of all things.") They're life's lessons for undesirable behavior, and you can harness their power to decrease your child's unwanted behaviors.

In the long term, natural consequences can be more effective than parent-imposed consequences; they're naturally closely related to the behavior and take place without any potential harm to the parent-child relationship. They're gifts to you: consequences that you don't have to implement, so your child won't associate that negativity with you.

When possible, point out the consequences of your child's behavior before it occurs: "If you go to sleep late, you'll have a hard time concentrating tomorrow." "If you tease your friend, she won't want to play with you." "If you don't study, you'll do badly on your test." "If it takes you too long to get dressed, you won't have time for pancakes for breakfast." Pointing it out will highlight the connection between the behavior and the consequence, so when it occurs, your child will be able to recognize that connection.

When those consequences arise, quash the desire to smugly say, "I told you so!" If you think your child isn't able to put two and two together, merely (and unemotionally) point out what happened as a result of his behavior and let him draw his own conclusions. He knows that you told him it would happen; don't rub his face in it. Instead, you can sympathize (when appropriate, and without validating the behavior): "You must be disappointed that this grade brings down your average."

You may also want to neutrally point it out when it arises again: "I know you have a big test tomorrow. Remember to study so that we don't have a repeat of last time." Just check your relationship with your child first, and only point it out if you think he'll be open to hearing it. If the consequence is obvious, your child may resent you for pointing it out ("I *knew* you would rub it in!"). This can harm your relationship and totally cancel out the benefits!

If your child does poorly on a major test after not studying enough, you may feel like sticking up for him and asking the teacher to find a way to raise his grade. If the grade is not actually unfair, don't interfere with the consequence! It's hard to watch him suffer, but don't try to make it up to him by taking him out for ice cream; that will undo the positive effects of the natural consequence.

However, sometimes the natural consequences that you've warned your kid about do not occur, prompting the dreaded gleeful "See, nothing happened!" She didn't study and still aced the test. He didn't wear a sweatshirt and wasn't cold. They played on top of the car and nobody fell off or dented anything. Now what?

You may be tempted to attach your own consequence, but that's likely to backfire. Instead, sit your child down and tell him why you warned him about the possible consequences: "I'm so happy it worked out for you, but I just want to let you know that procrastinating and not taking responsibility for your work can hurt you in the long run." "I love you and I don't want to see you get hurt when the irresponsibility catches up with you." If there are no natural consequences of a particular behavior (or if the consequences are unsafe), choose a different intervention to stop the behavior.

There are some times when you shouldn't allow your child to experience natural consequences: when his actions could harm him or someone else (like if he's climbing on the roof or trying to run over his sister with his bike) or if the consequences could be detrimental to him, but he doesn't care (like if he won't brush his teeth or refuses to eat anything but potato chips). In these cases, you can implement other behavior-change strategies.

Punishment in Action

Twelve-year-old Hazel is constantly butting heads with her ten-year-old brother, Sawyer. Today, Sawyer used Hazel's favorite gel pens without permission, so Hazel decided to pay him back by messing with his possessions.

Sawyer:	(*running up to Dad in tears*) Dad! Dad! Hazel trashed my room! She went through everything and threw all my stuff on the floor, and she broke my model plane… (*He dissolves into hysterics.*)
Dad:	(*already frustrated by the constant bickering*) She did *what?!* Okay, that does it. (*He storms up to Hazel's room, where she's attempting to hide behind the door.*)
Dad:	Hazel! How dare you destroy your brother's room! Get up right now. (*He hauls her up and marches her over to Sawyer's room.*)
Hazel:	But Dad, he touched my stuff first!
Dad:	He touched your stuff? Did he *ruin* your stuff? Look at this room! You destroyed it! You will stay here until every last bit of this room is cleaned up, and you will buy him a new model plane. And you will do his chores for the week.
Hazel:	No! No! I won't do it! That's so unfair! He never gets in trouble for touching my stuff. I am *not* cleaning this up. He deserved it! He's a jerk and I hate him! And I hate you! (*She stomps off to her own room and starts throwing things around in a fit of rage.*)
Dad:	(*following Hazel*) Excuse me? You do not talk to me like that!
Hazel:	I hate you! I hate this house! I wish you were all dead! (*She kicks her desk violently.*)
Dad:	(*grabbing Hazel's arm*) And *now* you are grounded until you learn to respect other people and property.

Both Dad and Hazel are left angry at themselves and each other, and Hazel likely hasn't learned anything from this encounter.

Let's examine what happened.

1. Dad's first fundamental error: parenting while angry.

2. Dad's first consequences (cleaning up the room and replacing the broken model) were specific, time-limited, meaningful, and connected to the infraction. Ten points for Dad!

3. The consequence of taking over Sawyer's chores was less effective. It's not related to the behavior, and it's too harsh for the "offense."

4. Dad continues to allow his emotions to take control of him, so he reacts strongly as Hazel reacts to the punishment.

5. Dad piles on more consequences as Hazel's behavior escalates, creating a downward spiral and power struggle.

Now, let's try that again—effectively this time.

Sawyer: (*running up to Dad in tears*) Dad! Dad! Hazel trashed my room! She went through everything and threw all my stuff on the floor, and she broke my model plane… (*He dissolves into hysterics.*)

Dad: (*takes a deep breath to steady himself and tamp down the rising anger*) Oh, no, Sawyer, that's awful, you worked really hard on that plane. Go play in the yard for a while and I'll take care of it.

Dad: (*in a controlled tone of voice*) Hazel, stand up. You made an enormous mess in Sawyer's room, and you broke that model plane that he worked so hard on.

Hazel: (*defiantly*) I don't care! He deserved it! He used my special pens without permission, and he mixed up all the colors. He's a stupid jerk and I hate him!

Dad: That's really upsetting. I know you don't like it when he touches your stuff. I'll talk to him about that. Hazel, destroying people's things is never okay. You need to calm down now, and we will discuss this when you are not so angry anymore.

[*Hazel slams the door, screaming about how unfair her life is. Thirty minutes later, when she's quieted down, Dad revisits the conversation.*]

Dad: I'm glad to see that you're calm now. I see that you were very upset that Sawyer used your pens. I talked to him about that. Even though he touched your stuff, that doesn't make it okay to destroy his stuff. Now, you need to go clean up every single part of his room, and you will buy him a new plane to replace the one you broke. There will be no screen time or playing with your friends until you are done.

Hazel: But Dad, I didn't mess up his whole room! Why should I clean up the whole thing?

Dad: That is the consequence that you are getting. You may not destroy people's things.

[*Hazel stomps off. After the cleanup is finished, Dad comes back to talk to Hazel again.*]

Dad: I'm proud of the way you cleaned up Sawyer's room! Now you can go out with your friends or get back to your screen time. Let's talk about what you can do the next time you're mad at him. Do you have any good ideas?

Hazel: (*still a little sullen*) Yeah. I can put a chain lock on my door so he can never get in again.

Dad: (*chuckling*) That would work to keep him out of your stuff. I think he'll still find ways to annoy you. How about coming to tell Mom or me about it? Do you have any other good ideas?

Hazel: I guess I can try.

Dad: Great. Let me know if you have any questions. I'm always ready to help you!

In this version of events, Hazel learns that some lines may not be crossed without consequences. Her relationship with Dad—and the atmosphere in the house—stays more positive, and Dad keeps his cool.

What did he do right?

1. **Mindfulness:** Dad takes a break and waits until he's calm to address the issue, so his emotions don't crowd out his rational mind. (Bonus: he calms Sawyer down, too.)

2. **Validation:** Dad validates Hazel's anger at Sawyer for touching her pens, even though her reaction was inappropriate. This deescalates the situation and helps Hazel get a hold on her emotions.

3. **Extinction** (we'll get to this skill soon!)**:** Dad remains focused on the issue at hand. He doesn't get sidetracked by Hazel's name-calling ("stupid jerk"), door-slamming, or screaming.

4. **Effectiveness:** Dad waits until Hazel is no longer out of control before giving her a consequence; the consequence is appropriate, specific, and meaningful. He also requires Hazel to overcorrect by cleaning the *entire* room after she cleans up what she wrecked. He motivates her to overcorrect by banning screen time and play time until the cleanup is finished. Furthermore, Dad does not harp on the behavior after the consequence ends. He moves on and is not overly critical, punitive, or angry, and he helps Hazel come up with replacement behaviors and a strategy for next time.

It's the same consequence, but with a totally different outcome thanks to effective parenting!

Extinction

Extinction is the process of removing all reinforcers—positive or negative—in response to a behavior. It's pointedly and deliberately ignoring the behavior; in fact, it's also known as *planned ignoring*. When the behavior gets no attention whatsoever, the child will stop (eventually).

Extinction is often effective for behaviors that can be ignored. This skill works well when you can tolerate the behavior (even when it escalates) and when it's not an extreme behavior that must be stopped immediately. It's a good go-to strategy when a child is acting out in an attention-seeking, inappropriate, immature, or annoying way (e.g., whining, tantruming, screaming). It should *not* be used when the behavior is harming or significantly bothering others.

Have you ever tried to get a snack or drink from a broken vending machine? First you press the button a bunch of times. Then you jab at the other buttons. Then you press the "coin return" button repeatedly. Then you give the machine a hearty shake, or even a kick. Finally, when you realize that the machine is really and truly broken, you walk away.

With extinction, you become that broken soda machine. Your child will try to push your buttons, usually at an increasingly frantic pace, but he'll eventually give up and go away.

You may have practiced extinction if you've ever sleep-trained a baby. With many sleep-training methods, even the gentler ones, parents are encouraged to let the baby cry for periods of time. While it's wrenching to hear the baby cry, over time he eventually cries for shorter and shorter periods as he learns that crying will not get him what he wants—to come out of his crib, to stay up longer, or to be rocked to sleep.

The How-Tos of Extinction

When your child starts the target behavior (interrupting, burping at the table, making annoying noises), put your skill into action.

Actively ignore the behavior. Remove yourself from the environment, if possible or necessary. If your child needs a reminder to behave appropriately, point out a replacement behavior and let him know that you'll be ignoring any further interaction. "When you ask politely—try, 'Please can I have a cookie after dinner?'—and use an inside voice, I will be ready to talk to you again." This step isn't always necessary; many behaviors can simply be ignored without any attention at all.

Beware of the *behavioral burst*: increased frequency or intensity in a bid for attention as your child gets more agitated or desperate. "Mom, stop ignoring me! You're the worst mom ever! I hate this house! I'm taking the cookie anyway!"

Continue ignoring even as the behavior escalates. It's to be expected! Remind yourself that he's attempting to push your buttons, and ignore him even when it's really hard. Wordlessly take the cookies from his hand and put them on a high shelf. Ignore his dramatic flailing and wailing. As long as nobody's getting hurt, stick with that ignoring (even though it won't be easy!).

If your child challenges your rule, *don't react.* Later—after the storm has died down—remind him about what happened and give an appropriate consequence, if necessary. "I know you were upset before, and it was not okay that you took a cookie before dinner. Tomorrow you will not be able to have a cookie at all."

If anyone is endangered by the child's reaction to extinction, calmly remove him from the situation with as little reinforcement as possible. "You are hurting your brother, so you will go into your room until you are calm." (If that is difficult, remove yourself and others instead.)

Remember that consistency is key! If you respond at all, that's intermittent reinforcement—and that's the type of reinforcement that's the hardest to break.

A valuable skill to help you stay calm through the (often stressful) extinction experience is a technique known as "broken record." When necessary, repeat yourself like a broken record for the duration of the extinction period. Choose a phrase and calmly repeat it (or a slight variation on it) every single time he goes for that cookie.

Mom:	Cookies are for after dinner.
Daniela:	But I really want one!
Mom:	I'm sorry, but cookies are for after dinner.
Daniela:	So I won't have one after dinner!
Mom:	We can only have cookies after dinner.
Daniela:	I'm taking one anyway!
Mom:	I already said that cookies are for after dinner.
Daniela:	You're the worst mom ever! Everyone else gets cookies whenever they want!
Mom:	In this house, we eat cookies after dinner.

Extinction is a process. It's (typically) not a one-time-use skill that works immediately. Again, it's like sleep-training; the baby doesn't usually learn to sleep after one night of training. Throughout the extinction process, you may want to keep track of its effectiveness. You can monitor the frequency, length, and intensity of the behavior to observe whether it's decreasing over time.

Extinction in Action

Back talk and disrespect are all too common in nine-year-old Dylan's house. He lashes out at his parents whenever he's frustrated or when they deny his requests. Mom and Dad tried a behavioral chart, which was only minimally effective, and consequences (sending Dylan to his room for back talk), which led to endless tantrums and more inappropriate language.

Today, Mom realized that Dylan's been getting a lot of attention for his back talk. She's decided to try extinction.

Dylan: Mom, I'm going out to play basketball with Joshua.

Mom: Did you finish your homework?

Dylan: It's only a little, I'll finish it later. It's getting dark and Joshua has to leave!

Mom: Sorry, honey, you know the rule. No playing outside until after homework.

Dylan: But that's the most idiotic rule ever! I always get my homework done anyway!

Mom: That's the rule. Dylan, that was disrespectful. I'm not going to respond to you when you talk that way. If you want to discuss the rules, we can do it when you're ready to speak respectfully.

Dylan: I hate that rule! Just let me go out this time! I need to get out of this stupid house!

Mom: I'm ready to listen when you speak respectfully.

Dylan: I don't have to listen to you! I can talk however I want to talk. And I'm going outside now!

Mom: *(continues what she was doing, without looking at Dylan)*

Dylan: Stop ignoring me! It's your fault; if you didn't make such lame rules, I wouldn't always fight about them.

Mom: *(walks into the living room and sits down on the couch)*

Dylan: (*following*) Mom! Mom! MOM! (*starts throwing pillows off the couch*) MOM! Listen to me!

Mom: (*continues reading her magazine*)

Dylan: I wish I had a different mom! This is the worst family! I'm going out now, and I don't care what you say!

Defiantly, Dylan storms out of the house (with some more choice expletives and door slamming).

Later, Mom calmly tells Dylan that he has lost his allowance because he defied her. (This was a previously agreed-upon consequence.)

Did you spot all of Mom's effective extinction skills?

1. She clearly stated that she would ignore the behavior (speaking disrespectfully).

2. She reminded him of the appropriate behavior ("I'm ready to listen when you speak respectfully").

3. She did not respond to increasingly heated language and threats during the behavioral burst.

4. She removed herself from the situation.

5. She continued to ignore Dylan, even when he openly disobeyed her.

6. She dealt appropriately with an unacceptable behavior (defiance) after the encounter ended and emotions died down.

Had Mom responded to any of Dylan's threats—and she probably had to bite her tongue really hard not to—she would have undone the effectiveness of extinction. Furthermore, she would have reinforced the behavior that finally got her to respond. If she'd done that, Dylan would revert to that behavior (throwing, threatening, swearing) a lot sooner the next time around.

Satiation

Satiation, the opposite of extinction, is a calmer strategy that can be quite effective. In DBT, it's the act of satiating, or filling up, your child's needs—attention, activities, food, drinks, sleep—giving him what he wants or needs *before* it becomes necessary. It's heading off the tantrum/fight/screaming fit before it ever happens.

The goal of satiation, like the other strategies in this chapter, is to stop a behavior. Often, the most effective starting point is to find the cause of the behavior and work to prevent it entirely.

Some children act out because they're looking for attention. Even "bad" attention is still attention. Kids may act out to be heard, seen, or noticed by their parents or siblings; they crave the attention and stimulation.

Your child is not necessarily actively seeking attention, though. For instance, when a toddler tantrums, he gets attention. After a few tantrums, he starts to subconsciously associate "tantrum" with "attention." On the other hand, if you give him just as much attention when he's *not* tantruming, the "tantrum = attention" association doesn't form.

Behavioral triggers can also be more biological: hunger, thirst, fatigue. You've probably practiced satiation on your kids as babies and toddlers. You may have learned their usual sleeping and eating habits and adjusted your schedule according to that, feeding the baby before he screamed from hunger or putting the toddler down for a nap before he melted down in exhaustion.

Satiation for big-kid behavior follows the same concept: figure out what's causing your child's behavior, and do what it takes to prevent that. Once that need is satiated, he's no longer motivated to misbehave in order to get what he wants. The benefits are twofold: his need is fulfilled (without drama!), and he learns that he does not need to act out to have his needs met.

The How-Tos of Satiation

To practice satiation, you'll need to do some detective work. (Your Observe and Describe skills will come in handy here.)

Pay attention to the circumstances surrounding your child's behavior. Sometimes it's easy to find the cause: your child will let you know in no uncertain terms that she's "starving" or "sooooo bored" or "exhausted." At other times, it can be harder to pinpoint.

Identify the times when your child tends to misbehave. Is it after school? During the morning rush? On long weekends?

You may notice a pattern.

- Does he come home ravenous and crabby? Have dinner or a snack ready when the kids walk in the door.

- Do they fight every Sunday afternoon when they're bored? Draw up a schedule for the day, enroll them in an activity, or prepare something fun to do.

- Does your preschooler hit the baby when he's feeling neglected? Invite him to snuggle next to you and read a book while you hold his little sister and praise him to the sky for being so gentle.

- Does "witching hour" come immediately before bedtime? Move bedtime up by half an hour or designate quiet reading time.

- Is pre-dinnertime prime meltdown time? Serve dinner a little earlier or put out a healthy "appetizer" to stave off hunger-induced tantrums.

This will probably take some practice, planning, and fine-tuning. If you know that your child starts following you around, whining, asking questions, crying, or fighting the *instant* you pick up the phone or go to prepare dinner, try satiation first. Fill up his "tank" with attention. Need fifteen minutes of quiet? First sit down and give your child your undivided attention for fifteen minutes. You may be pleasantly surprised to see that he'll occupy himself once you've satiated his need for attention.

Obviously, satiation needs to be provided within reason. You cannot (and should not) anticipate every possible trigger and tiptoe around trying to keep your child happy at all times; you'll wind up a resentful parent with a coddled kid.

As always, balance is important. Satiation isn't a skill that can (or should) be used in every encounter. It isn't catering to their every whim! It's most helpful when you can pinpoint the cause of the behavior, then find an easy, doable way to stop it before it starts. Identifying the triggers and stopping them before they start can mean the difference between full-on tantrum mode and slightly-grouchy-but-manageable mode.

Like every strategy, satiation has pros and cons. One major advantage: it provides similar relief to extinction, minus the behavioral burst. On the flip-side, a disadvantage of satiation is that you may wind up providing more reinforcers than you'd like. Weigh those pros and cons before using satiation (and any other strategy).

Satiation in Action

Seven-year-old Olivia comes home from school every day and promptly creates chaos. She melts down. She picks fights. She whines. She refuses to do her homework. She's becoming increasingly unhappy, and so is the rest of the family.

Mom has tried pretty much everything and is at her wits' end.

Finally, Mom sits down and examines Olivia's behavior. She notices that Olivia tends to melt down at other times, too, and keeps track of those times. Over the span of a few days, she observes that Olivia gets whiny and upset around mealtimes. Plus, she's irritable when it's noisy, constantly screaming at everyone to be quiet and get away from her *or else*.

Since Olivia has a long, noisy day followed by a long, noisy bus ride, Mom realizes that she's melting down after school simply because she's hungry, tired, and overstimulated. Coming home to a bustling house—especially when her baby brother is crying or when Mom wants her to do her homework right away—is enough to send her over the edge.

The next day, Mom is ready. She lays out a healthy-but-yummy snack, meets Olivia at the door, and directs her to a quiet space to enjoy her snack in peace.

Olivia is slightly startled by the change in routine, but ten minutes later, she's ready to talk about her day.

Mom's not spoiling Olivia; she's helping her stay on top of her emotions and giving the whole family the opportunity to enjoy peaceful afternoons.

Roadblocks to Punishment, Extinction, and Satiation

When it comes to hot-button topics like punishment, you may encounter thoughts or feelings that can interfere with your effectiveness. Below are some common roadblocks to punishment, extinction, and satiation—and more effective thoughts to replace them with. You can also download the Chapter 7 Roadblock Cards at http://www.newharbinger.com/46868.

Roadblock (the statement)	Detour (the solution)
Punishment is cruel, mean, and outdated. I could never punish my child.	Effective punishment is not punitive or callous; it is a valuable parenting strategy, when used properly.
Kids need to be punished and put in their place! We coddle our kids too much. They need to know who's boss.	Punishment *is* necessary—in moderation, and done effectively: not with anger, not to prove who's in charge, and not in a controlling manner.

My kids will hate me for punishing them, just like I hated my parents for punishing me!	While your kids may be upset by punishment, when you punish effectively, it benefits them in many different ways and actually helps children feel more secure and loved.
It's just not my personality to impose consequences on my kids. Let them learn naturally.	You do not need to be (and, truthfully, shouldn't be) the stereotypical stern disciplinarian to use consequences effectively. Every parent has the ability to punish, regardless of his or her personality or parenting style. If you feel like you can't, exercise your *opposite action* skill and do it anyway!
Ignoring my child is rude. I don't want her to think that it's okay to ignore people.	Using extinction skills does not mean ignoring your child; it is ignoring her inappropriate behavior.
How can I let him act that way and ignore it? He'll think he can get away with anything!	Aim for balance; using extinction does not mean that you can ignore every behavior and hope that it goes away. Use it strategically, effectively, and sensibly.
Satiation is just a fancy name for spoiling.	Using satiation is not spoiling your child, as long as you don't try to prevent every single behavior. When used effectively, your child may not even notice that you're doing anything different!

Overview: Change Strategies

In this and the previous chapter, we covered seven different techniques for changing behavior. All of them are valuable and useful in different situations and relationships, and they can all be used to address the same behavior (just not all at once!).

When your child is acting out, assess the severity of the behavior, the state of your relationship, your personality, and your child's personality when choosing how to address the behavior. For example, if your child is hitting when he's upset, you may deal with the behavior in one of seven ways. Your options are listed below.

Positive reinforcement	For every two-hour period that he doesn't hit anyone, he earns a sticker, with a prize after fifteen stickers.
Negative reinforcement	When he hits, tell him that if he continues hitting, he will have to leave the playroom where everyone is playing.
Positive punishment	When he hits, send him to his room for a time-out.
Negative punishment	When he hits, he loses a toy or privilege.
Natural consequences	Say, "Your sister doesn't want to play with you because you hit her."
Extinction	Walk away from him when he hits you. (And only you; do not ignore when he hits his siblings.)
Satiation	Identify the time of day when he's most likely to hit. Provide him with a quiet space or with extra attention, praise, or activities before and during that time.

While these skills can all be adapted to address various behaviors, in many situations and circumstances, one skill may be more appropriate and effective than the others.

Which Skill When?

Problem Behavior	Recommended Strategy
You tell your child to come inside. He yells and screams that it's not fair and continues crying and complaining once he's in the house.	Extinction. Ignore the verbal tantrum and wait for it to blow over.
Your child is resisting bedtime, procrastinating, and constantly coming out of bed.	Positive reinforcement. Implement a chart or reward, praise her for getting into bed on time, and offer a special story if she's in bed by a specified time.
Your child screams at her brother to "get out of here" and throws her video game controller at him.	Negative punishment. She loses the remainder of her screen time.
Your child gets needy and clingy whenever you start cooking dinner or spending time with another child.	Satiation. Set up a "special time" slot or date every day or a few times a week for one-on-one attention.
Your child is teasing and bothering his siblings while they're playing outside.	Negative reinforcement. If he continues to bother his siblings, he has to go back inside.
Your child turns destructive when she's angry and purposely breaks a dinner plate.	Positive punishment. She helps you find a replacement plate and pays for it out of her allowance.
Your child doesn't come home on time when you're waiting to start an activity, leave on an outing, or give out a treat.	Natural consequences. He didn't get home in time; he misses the activity/outing/treat.

All of the skills you've learned in chapters 6 and 7 play crucial roles in effective parenting. Some are more effective for certain situations, certain times, and certain personalities; each skill is valuable in different ways. Depending on the circumstances, any one—or a combination—of these strategies can be effective.

With practice (and mindfulness!), you'll learn when and how to use each strategy for short- and long-term effectiveness. Don't worry if it takes time and some failed attempts; the trial-and-error process will help you move forward with confidence. In the next chapter, you'll learn about setting and implementing limits, which will help you take stock of your skill toolbox and figure out a system that works for you and your family. You're doing great—keep it up!

CHAPTER 8

Setting, Implementing, and Maintaining Limits

"That child needs limits!"

—the older, disapproving woman who (unfortunately)
witnessed your kid's epic meltdown

You've heard it before: kids need limits. You've probably nodded your head sagely in agreement. Maybe you've even said it yourself. But when it comes down to setting limits, things tend to get tricky and doubt begins to set in. *Why are limits important? How do I know if my limits are as unreasonable as my teen claims they are? When do I need to set limits? How can I set limits that work for me and for my kids? Is it ever okay to change or break a limit?*

Sometimes it seems easier to just let the kids do what they want and hope for the best.

That may be a great short-term solution—no tension, no frustration, no arguments, parents and kids are happy—but long term, it leads to undisciplined children, poor boundaries, and lifelong issues, which get in the way of your ultimate goals.

Limit setting can be challenging, especially because kids love to test those limits. Don't give up—effective limit setting is a powerful change strategy when you have the skills in your toolbox and the motivation to use them successfully.

In this chapter, you'll learn:

- Why it's necessary to set limits

- When to set limits

- What you need to know before setting limits

- How to set limits (even when your kids fight them)
- How to be both consistent and flexible: a dialectical balance
- How to overcome obstacles to limit setting

Why Is Limit Setting Important?

Limits are vital to a child's health and growth. No child is born with the inherent ability to set limits on his own behavior, and if he's not taught, he will have difficulty navigating adult life and limiting himself. A lack of limits often leads to self-destructive behaviors like alcohol and drug abuse, but it also presents less extreme challenges: an inability to refrain from buying something out of budget, difficulty standing up to peer pressure, or trouble controlling urges.

Emotionally dysregulated children will typically not develop the ability to regulate their impulses as they mature; limits will teach them to do this as necessary. These children tend to test limits and break boundaries due to their difficulty with impulse control and heightened emotional urges. While you may be tempted to stretch or suspend those limits to accommodate your child's sensitivity (or to avoid yet another confrontation), he needs those limits. Appropriate, effective limit setting, balanced with plenty of soothing and validation, will empower him to take on the world.

When Should I Set Limits?

Limits are the "stop sign" of parenting; a limit is the point up until where a behavior is encouraged or acceptable. Proper limits define the boundaries of appropriate and permissible within every individual family.

Parents must set limits on various everyday aspects of their children's lives. Limits clearly communicate your expectations to your children and allow for smooth day-to-day running of the household. Introducing and reinforcing limits in early childhood helps children learn that there are boundaries in the home and allows parents to shape their children's behavior as they grow.

For younger children, limit setting is most important in situations that arise frequently—even daily—in the home. These times and situations may include:

- Bedtime, including routines ("After you brush your teeth and clean up your room, we can read a book and sing a song") and schedules ("If you are in bed at eight, you can read until lights out at 8:15.")

- Mealtime, including manners ("Use your fork"; "No reading, toys, or electronics at the table"; "Chew quietly with your mouth closed"; "Ask to be excused before you leave the table"), food consumption ("I expect you to eat at least half of your serving"; "You have to try at least one bite of everything before asking for something else"; "Start with a small portion, and if you're hungry you can have seconds"), and meal choices ("Choose one protein"; "If you don't like dinner, you can help yourself to a yogurt and rice cakes or make a sandwich.")

- Playtime, with guidelines for length of time spent playing ("Please be inside at 7:00"), organization ("Put away the toy or game before you take out another one"), and playing together ("Now it's his turn; it will be your turn in five minutes"; "If you don't want to share a toy, put it away before your friend comes over—if it's out, you will need to share it.")

- Gifts, with limits and expectations related to the frequency of gift-giving ("We give presents for birthdays, holidays, graduations, and other special events and as rewards for specific behaviors or accomplishments"), appropriate people to accept gifts from ("It's okay to take a gift from Grandma; it's not okay to accept a present from a stranger"), and the proper way to accept a gift ("Say thank you, even if you don't like it"; "Write a thank-you note promptly.")

- Snacks and treats, including defining "anytime" snacks versus "sometimes" snacks ("You may always help yourself to fruit, vegetables, string cheese, or crackers"; "These cookies are for an after-school snack"; "We're saving those candies for a special occasion") and appropriate snack times and amounts ("No eating half an hour before dinnertime, except vegetables"; "Check if there's another package before you finish it"; "You can have fruit up until bedtime but not after bedtime.")

- Language, such as words and phrases that are acceptable and unacceptable ("You may not call your brother names; this includes 'stupid' or anything else that upsets him"; "We do not use that word in this house.")

- Screen time limits, such as how often ("You can have the iPad twice a week"; "No screens during family time"; "You can watch your show if you're finished with your homework by then"), how much ("No more than half an hour of screen time per day"), and how to earn or lose time ("Extra screen time is okay on long car trips"; "If you finish cleaning your room by 5:00, you can play an extra game on my phone.")

- Safety, including personal safety ("If someone hurts you or touches you in a way you don't like, you should tell me or another adult right away and we won't be mad"; "Do not keep any secrets from your parents"), home safety ("No climbing on the furniture"; "Stay away from the stove"; "No touching the matches"), and outdoor safety ("You must wear your helmet and appropriate safety gear while riding your bike, rollerblading, or playing sports"; "Stop and walk your bike across the street"; "You may ride from the corner until the Smiths' house.")

For teens, additional (or adapted) limits are necessary:

- Curfew: "Be home (and inside!) by ten."

- Supervision: "You can sleep over at your friends' houses if there is a parent present."

- Clothing: "If you want that designer brand, you'll have to pay for it yourself or earn it with chores"; "Short shorts are unacceptable"; "I reserve the right to veto your clothing choices."

- Recreational activities: "I'm happy to bring you and your friends to the bowling alley"; "You may not go to the beach alone after dark."

As you will read in this chapter, several factors—societal norms, morals, religion, family values, and individual circumstances—influence the hows, whens, whys, and wheres of limit setting.

What to Consider When Setting Limits

Setting limits can be a balancing act; it's most effective when done thoughtfully and proactively rather than in response to an ongoing situation. You'll need to consider several factors before putting limits into place. It's best to address these points and questions with your spouse, co-parent, or any other involved party to ensure that you present a united front to your child. Below, we'll explore several factors to consider when preparing to set limits, starting with your relationship with your child.

The Parent-Child Relationship

Before creating and enforcing limits, take a good, hard look at your current relationship with your child; use your mindfulness Observe and Describe skills. No child consciously likes being limited, and it's important to strike a healthy balance of positivity and negativity. Your child will be more receptive to limits when she lives in an encouraging, affectionate environment with plenty of positivity and a pleasant relationship with her parents.

John Gottman and Robert Levenson (2002) defined the ideal "magic" ratio of positive to negative communications in marriages as five positives to every negative. Applying this to the parent-child relationship, the magic ratio is five positives to every negative, five "yeses" to every "no," five enjoyable interactions to every less-pleasant experience. The positives—which can be as easy as playing a short game together, asking her about her day, listening to his joke, or having a positive conversation—will pad your relationship with your child, cushioning the blow of limit setting. (Plus, when your child protests—as she likely will—that you "never let her do anything" and that "every other parent lets their kid do that," you'll be secure in the knowledge that your relationship is positive for the overwhelming majority of the time!)

Ask yourself: *Is our relationship mostly positive right now? Do I have evidence that my child feels loved by me (says, "I love you," hugs me back, shares feelings with me, comes to me for advice)?*

POSITIVE-NEGATIVE RATIO EXERCISE

Keep a log—a physical log, on a piece of paper or electronic device—of your positive and negative interactions with your child. After a few days, review the log to see if you're really as positive (or negative!) as you think you are and if you need to change. In addition to evaluating your relationship status, this exercise will enhance your awareness during parent-child interactions and help you reinforce your own actions, leading to increased positivity and effective change.

Your Emotional State

Attempting to set limits when you're upset is practically begging for a blowup. When you're in an emotional state, your emotions dictate your thoughts and behaviors; this often leads to limits that are extreme, punitive, and ineffective. Furthermore, emotions tend to send strong messages to children—stronger than those of words—so even if you use all the right words and phrases, your child will walk away from the interaction believing that you set the limit because you were fed up or angry at him, not because you care about him.

Check your own emotional state—mindfully!—before working on limit setting (or any other form of discipline, for that matter). If you're upset, wait until you're calm and aware to be sure that you're doing what works rather than acting on your emotions (or ask your spouse to take over). Even if you lose an opportunity to set limits, holding off due to your emotional state is more effective long term than attempting to discipline in a heightened emotional state.

Ask yourself (or your spouse or another person whom you trust): *Am I regulated enough to put a limit in place now? Are my emotions too intense right now?* (If you're unsure, it's better to err on the side of caution; if possible, have your spouse step in to take over.)

Your Child's Capabilities

Every child is different. The fact that nine-year-olds on *MasterChef Junior* can chop and flambé like pros doesn't mean your nine-year-old is ready to cook scrambled eggs; the fact that your sister's four-year-old can handle disappointment without a tantrum doesn't mean that your four-year-old can do it; the fact that your older child was allowed to cross the street alone at age ten doesn't mean that your current (dreamier) ten-year-old is responsible enough to cross.

We often look at our children through various lenses—our own childhood experience, their siblings or relatives, friends and neighbors—rather than at their individual temperament, strengths, and weaknesses.

Look at *your* child and her capabilities and limitations, not at the expectations of what a child this age "should" be doing. (Don't forget the evils of "should"—remember your dialectics!) Sometimes, we expect our children to be able to do things that we've never taught them to do; they may need explicit instruction in certain skills that some kids develop on their own. If you tell your child to be home at a certain time but fail to equip him with a watch, good time-management skills, or the ability to ask an adult for the time, your expectation is not reasonable.

Ask yourself: *Is this limit appropriate to his developmental stage and personal capabilities?*

Existing Limits

"Pick your battles." It's one of those golden rules of parenting. Consider which situations are most in need of limits at the moment: if your child needs limits related to his aggression or back talk, you may want to loosen your expectations and limits related to his chores, bedtime, or eating habits.

Too many limits can become punitive, which often leads to a self-punitive attitude in the child: *I can't keep up with these expectations, there must be something wrong with me, I deserve to be punished.* Excessive limits can lead to a child's feeling resentful, restricted, unaccepted, and unloved; developing a self-critical perspective; and being punitive toward others. An overload of expectations or a constant barrage of limits will also lead to an unbalanced parent-child relationship. Be sure that your limits are reasonable and necessary before implementing them. After introducing the limit, mindfully observe your child's reactions and his abilities to ensure that he has the skills and capabilities to follow the limit.

Ask yourself: *What limits do I currently have in place? Is this specific limit too much for my child?*

The Parameters

Kids, like dogs, are highly adept at sniffing out fear. (Or, to put it more sweetly, they're sensitive to your emotions…and they're experts at detecting your weak spots.) Define your limit for yourself first and come prepared for the interaction (and the ensuing pushback); be clear and confident. Your kids will be able to tell if you're serious or if you're ill-equipped to stand up to their negotiations.

Ask yourself: *Am I prepared? What are my specific conditions and expectations?*

Your Motivation

Again, be mindful: be aware of your own motive and rationale in setting this limit. Are you setting the limit to prove that you're the one in charge? Are you setting the limit because you want him to behave like that angelic neighbor kid (whose mom is just a little too smug for your taste)? Are you setting the limit because you love her and want what's best for her—and this limit will help her grow?

Ask yourself: *Why am I setting this limit?*

Context

Before setting a limit, it's important to do your homework; find out if your limit is reasonable and appropriate or if it will lead to justified resentment or social ostracization. Consider the whole child based on societal norms, community, culture, family values, and his specific circumstances (all of which, as you know, change constantly). Discuss the potential limit with your spouse or an objective (and informed) party, but remember to trust your parental instincts.

Ask yourself: *Is this limit appropriate given my child's personal and social particularities and norms?*

Time and Place

Timing is everything. Location, location, location. The clichés are overused for a reason! The best time and place to set a limit is in a quiet, private environment when you and your child are calm. Ideally, both parents should present it as a united front (though consider your parent-child relationship; at times it may be most effective if the parent who has a better relationship with the child sets the limit alone).

Of course, there will be times when it's virtually impossible to set your limits in that ideal setting; try to get as close to those conditions as possible. Pull your child over to a quiet corner; give him a few minutes to cool down; wait until she finishes her homework. A stressed, tired, hungry, or rushing child will not be receptive to limit setting!

Ask yourself: *Is now a good time to have this conversation with my child? Who is watching or listening? Is he on his way out the door? Is she highly emotional at the moment?*

How to Set, Maintain, and Communicate Limits

When you launch a limit-setting interaction, knowing exactly what to do and how to do it will help you be effective, efficient, and firm (yet loving!). Here's how:

Stand close to your child. Having a conversation across the room or yelling to a child from the bottom of the stairs will hinder an effective exchange; your child is more likely to respond when he sees that you are actually invested in the conversation.

Crouch or sit when appropriate. Assert your authority and stand nearby— just not in a threatening manner. Don't loom over your child, which can be overwhelming and intimidating; going below the child's eye level by crouching or kneeling will make him feel safer and less defensive.

Make eye contact. Continuous eye contact shows that you are serious and committed.

Stay focused. Now is not the time to check your email, converse with your spouse, change the baby's diaper, or remind your child about the chore that he hasn't finished; remember to do *one thing in the moment!*

State the limit briefly and clearly. Stick to the script! Don't leave room for interpretation; don't lecture; don't waffle back and forth ("You need to be home by seven" rather than "Come home in about half an hour").

Give a concise and clear explanation. "You need to come in at seven so you'll have enough time to get ready for bed." Don't expect your child to "see the light" and suddenly become agreeable once she sees your reasoning; be prepared for negotiation attempts and pleading. (As a parent, you certainly don't "owe" your child an explanation, but when it's straightforward, offering a brief explanation can be more effective as it shows your child that you're not enforcing a limit "just to be mean.")

State the consequences. Let your child know why he should listen, or what's in it for him: "If you stay up late, you won't be able to concentrate in school tomorrow" (natural consequence) or "if you come back late, you'll have to come in earlier tomorrow/you'll lose your screen time" (parent-imposed consequence). When a child is generally responsive to limits, a consequence may not be necessary, and stating the natural consequences may be enough so that the child understands your motivation. (If you need help with consequences, head back to chapter 7 for a refresher.)

Follow through. If your child sees that the stated consequences are not enforced, why should she bother following your instructions? Be prepared to enforce the consequences.

Don't be afraid of "no." It's a clear, definitive word, and there's nothing wrong with using it. (So when your child starts the negotiations, don't hesitate to say, "The answer is no" rather than "That's not a good idea" or "I said what I said, and we're not discussing it!")

For maximum effectiveness, communicate limits in the following ways:

- **Softly and gently.** Use a soft tone, especially at the beginning of the conversation to avoid an immediate defensive reaction (still, be prepared for your child to respond with "Stop yelling at me!"). Believe it or not, your children will hear you best when you speak softly *and* assertively.

- **With balanced emotion** (even—or especially—if your child's emotions escalate). It's okay to feel the emotion, just use it effectively (bonus: it shows your child how to regulate his emotions, too!). Take a break and a breath to collect yourself if you're experiencing an intense emotion.

- **Nonjudgmentally.** Watch your posture, gesture, and tone (and remember your mindfulness "how" skills!); avoid sarcasm and phrases like "Are you serious?"

- **Lovingly.** Use explicit expressions of love: "I'm not saying no because I'm angry at you or because I don't want you to have fun; I'm saying no because that's what's best for you right now." (You can still expect your child to question it and get upset; don't worry, she's getting the message loud and clear!)

- **Confidently** (in appearance and speech). Even if you're not feeling confident, act confident! Don't hem and haw or say, "I think that what you're doing might not be such a good idea…"

- **Effectively.** Focus on doing what works. Are you getting stuck on principle or doing what's truly best for your child? Are you enforcing bedtime on a late summer evening because "bedtime is bedtime" or because your child really needs to go to sleep at that time in order to function the next day?

- **Single-mindedly.** Don't get sidetracked. Stay focused on the topic at hand and let go of power struggles. Lay out the facts, the conditions, and the consequences, even as your child veers off-topic. (Avoid conversations like this: "If you don't let me go out with my friends, I won't do my homework!" "Oh yes you will do your homework, young lady! And don't take that tone with me!")

- **Realistically.** Avoid empty threats and consequences that you cannot realistically enforce. When you're about to leave for a weeklong vacation—with the car packed and everyone ready to go—telling your sulky teen that he'll have to stay home if he doesn't change his attitude is simply not a realistic warning.

But they just don't listen! Wouldn't it be lovely if we did everything right and the kids smiled sweetly and did exactly as you said?

Yeah, real life doesn't work that way. They are still children, they have opinions and very determined minds of their own, and they will not necessarily respond positively to your limit setting. Ever heard of "testing your limits"?

If (when!) your kid pushes back when you set limits, try these strategies:

Touch. Use touch when appropriate—take him by the hand, touch him on the shoulder—for an extra level of connection, to get his attention, and to show that you are serious. Use caution: do not hurt your child (sometimes that "firm touch" may get a little too firm when you're feeling frustrated). This strategy generally works best with younger children; teens typically need more personal space and may get agitated if you invade theirs (know your child!).

Redirect. If your child is stuck on the "unfairness" of your limit, move on to a new activity or topic of conversation. This tends to work well with young children. (Some kids are very inflexible and will get even more frustrated if you try to distract them; consider using a different strategy if your child isn't receptive to redirection.)

Offer choices. Your limit may be more palatable if your child has a say in the matter. "Would you like to do your homework before or after dinner?" "It's time to get dressed now. Do you want the blue shirt or the purple dress?" Allowing her to choose helps her feel more in control of her life.

Reinforce the positive. Praise your child immediately when he listens—even if it's just a tiny step in the right direction.

Planned ignoring. Use your extinction skill from chapter 7. After stating the limit and its consequences, tell your child that the discussion is closed and that you will be ignoring any further debate, then follow through. Don't engage in any back and forth; ignore the threats, comments, attempts at diversion, or escalation (as long as nobody is being harmed). Stay focused and mindful. Responding at any point will reinforce the behavior intermittently, which will make your next attempt at planned ignoring futile!

Broken record. Yes, the same broken record from extinction. Repeat yourself as many times as necessary, no matter what your child responds. Use the same mellow tone and lack of emotion.

> *You:* It's time for bed.
>
> *Your child:* But I'm hungry!
>
> *You:* It's bedtime now. Good night.
>
> *Your child:* I forgot to do my homework!
>
> *You:* But now it's time for bed.
>
> *Your child:* You're so mean!
>
> *You:* It's time for bed.
>
> *Your child:* Stop saying that!

Be mindful of your child's reactions. Listen to him and pay attention; if he is truly struggling with the limit, he may need to be taught additional skills or you may need to be flexible and reconsider the terms.

Limit Setting in Action

Most limit setting takes place in regular, everyday scenarios. What would you do in this one?

Here's the scene: Mom's on the phone. (Let's assume it's a fairly important call.) Eight-year-old Lucas saunters into the kitchen in search of cookies.

The ensuing conversation could go two ways: ineffectively or effectively.

Lucas:	Hey Mom. Can I have a cookie?
Mom:	(*holding up a finger and whispering*) It's almost dinnertime.
	[*Mom is distracted and unable to give her attention to Lucas. She doesn't give him a clear answer; she assumes he knows that "almost dinnertime" means "no cookie."*]
Lucas:	I want a cookie! I'm starving!
Mom:	(*whispering a little louder now*) I said it's almost dinnertime.
	[*Mom still has not answered Lucas clearly.*]
Lucas:	You said I could have a cookie after school!
Mom:	(*muting the phone*) Lucas! Can't you see I'm on the phone? I said cookies after school, but now it's almost dinnertime!
	[*Mom is frustrated, allowing her emotions to heat up, and using a critical tone, which puts Lucas on the defensive. She is still distracted by her call.*]
Lucas:	I'm taking a cookie. (*heads to the cookie jar*)
	[*Lucas is taking advantage of Mom's distraction, attempting to show that he's in control, and testing Mom's limits.*]
Mom:	(*to caller*) Hang on, this is getting out of hand. (*to Lucas*) Lucas! That's enough! You are going straight to bed without dinner if this continues!
	[*Mom's emotion levels are rising, which—because change is transactional—leads to Lucas's emotions escalating; she issues an empty and unrealistic threat, turning the encounter into a power struggle.*]
Lucas:	(*voice escalating*) Why are you yelling at me? You said I could have cookies after school!
Mom:	I'm not yelling! I said no cookies! Why can't you just listen? Everyone else will get a cookie after dinner, but

you won't, because you're being disrespectful! Now get out of the kitchen before you get another consequence!

[*"I'm not yelling" invalidates Lucas's perspective; Mom never said "no cookies" until this moment. She is criticizing Lucas and comparing him to his siblings. She did not tell him that there would be consequences if he takes a cookie.*]

Lucas: I hate you! You're so mean! I'm not eating your disgusting dinner anyway!

Mom: You'd better believe that you're going to eat dinner, or you won't get cookies ever again!

[*Mom gets sidetracked by Lucas's threats and disrespect and continues to make empty threats, trying to regain control and quell her feelings of helplessness.*]

Lucas: (*storms off in a huff*)

Well, *that* ended well, didn't it? Here's how Mom could have handled the situation more effectively:

Lucas: Hey Mom. Can I have a cookie?

Mom: (*asks caller to hold for a moment*) Hi, sweetie. No, I'm sorry, it's almost dinnertime; you can't have a cookie now. If you have a cookie now, you won't have room for dinner.

[*Mom gives Lucas her attention and uses a term of endearment to decrease the potential for emotional escalation. She states the limit clearly and concisely, in a gentle way, with a clear explanation.*]

Lucas: But I'm so hungry!

Mom: I can help you find something healthy to eat. Would you like an apple or a tangerine?

[*Mom validates Lucas's hunger and offers a choice, which gives Lucas a sense of control.*]

Lucas: (*stomping foot*) I don't want a stupid fruit! You said I could have cookies after school!

Mom:	(*to caller*) I'm sorry, I'm going to have to call you back in a few minutes. (*to Lucas, walking over to him*) I understand that you're hungry; you had a long day. You can have a cookie after dinner. If you want a cookie after dinner, you'll have to wash your hands and eat something healthy now. You decide.

[Mom gets physically close, nonthreateningly, to Lucas and devotes her full attention—one-mindfully—to the situation and stays on track despite Lucas's disrespectful tone and his attempts at veering off topic. She states the limit clearly again, with a reinforcer for Lucas if he listens.]

Lucas:	Pleeeeease can I have a cookie now? I promise I'll eat my whole dinner.
Mom:	No, Lucas. You can't have a cookie now. It's almost dinnertime. If you wash your hands and eat something healthy now, you can have a cookie after dinner.

[Mom stays on topic and repeats herself in a soft yet assertive tone, broken-record style.]

Lucas:	(*sulkily*) Fine. I'll eat a tangerine.
Mom:	Great! That's a healthy choice. I'm so proud that you made that decision maturely. Go wash your hands and get a tangerine from the fridge.

[Mom immediately praises Lucas's positive behavior and follows through.]

Consistency and Flexibility

Like everything in parenting, limit setting requires a healthy balance between two concepts that seem to be opposites: consistency and flexibility. You'd think that they can't peacefully coexist: after all, if you're consistently consistent, there's no room to be flexible; if you're flexible, where's the consistency?

That's where the dialectics come in once again. You can be consistent *and* flexible, firm *and* adaptable, stable *and* accommodating.

You just have to know how.

Consistency

Consistency is important in child raising for several reasons.

Children, especially those with emotion regulation difficulties, thrive on structure and predictability; they perform better and respond better when they know what to expect.

Consistency helps parents maintain limits; if a child sees that there's room for negotiations—and manages to successfully negotiate changes—he will attempt to fight the limits every time. Children will use inconsistency to their advantage; they will often approach the parent who they know is more likely to give in, so be sure to always present a united front, parenting as a team!

When you're consistent in your parenting, it leads to positive change and behavior modification. (Imagine this: your boss wants to eliminate cell phone use at meetings. If he consistently addresses every instance of mid-meeting usage and nobody "gets away with it," you and your colleagues will stop attempting to use your cell phones, won't you?)

Consistency gives power and meaning to your words; without consistency and follow-through, your words become meaningless.

Flexibility

If consistency is so great, then why do we need flexibility?

Though the concepts may seem to be at odds, *flexibility* is not an antonym of *consistency*. (The opposite of flexibility is rigidity; the opposite of consistency is unpredictability.) While consistency is important in parenting, flexibility is equally important—when used effectively.

Flexibility allows us—and our children, who learn from our example—to deal with pressure. Think of trees in a storm; the strong, unyielding oak tree is more likely to crack in high wind than the supple willow tree, which bends but does not snap.

Here's why flexibility is important:

Change is the only constant: our children and circumstances are constantly changing, so we need to be prepared to change accordingly.

While many approaches emphasize the importance of consistency, consistency, consistency, focusing on only one extreme is generally unrealistic and not necessarily effective. The consistency-only model works well for pet training; children are far more emotionally complex and need to see that their parents are understanding and willing to work with them. Any one-sided approach is anti-dialectic; balancing consistency with flexibility is important to develop healthy, wholesome children.

Flexibility is one of the traits we'd like our children to display! An inflexible person has difficulty adapting to changes in schedule, environment, people, rules, and other circumstances—which, as we all know, are inevitable—and life's little (and not so little) surprises.

Parents make mistakes—after all, we are human beings. You (and your children) will fare better if you are flexible; plus, when a parent acknowledges that he made a mistake and apologizes, that's a powerful lesson for the child (and tends to lead to more respect and mimicking on the child's part).

When we are flexible, we validate our children's needs; flexibility illustrates our love and shows that we understand their viewpoints and take them seriously.

In families with more than one child, it can be tempting to use the same skills on all of them—after all, it worked for the oldest!—but you'll need flexibility to parent children with different temperaments and needs.

Now, here's the million-dollar question: *How can I be flexible and consistent at the same time?*

Every parent and every family must determine—mindfully—where and when they are willing to be flexible and where and when consistency is key.

You can use the Model of Flexibility (inspired by Gottman and Silver's [1999] two-oval compromise method for problem solving) to define your personal limits.

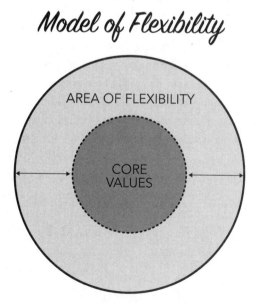

The center circle (with the dotted line) represents your core values, such as family norms, societal norms, and religious norms. It's your vision for how your family operates. If, for example, one of your core values is neatness and cleanliness, you might use the model to find the flexibility balance regarding your child's messy room. In that case, the center circle can contain the way you want her to keep her room, based on your core value: clothes in the closet, floor clear, minimal dust, sheets changed regularly.

The solid outer circle is your firm do-not-cross limit: no old or rotten food, no mess spillover to other rooms, no piles of dirty clothes on the floor.

The donut-shaped area between the two lines is the area of flexibility. That's where everything between your inner circle and your outer limit falls. It's not part of your ideal vision, but you may be willing to tolerate it: a stack of clothes on a chair, clutter under the bed, dusty furniture, open or messy drawers, an abundance of knickknacks.

Aim to keep the inner circle as small as possible. It's surrounded by a dotted line because it's not as definite as the outer circle. The goal is to have a large area of flexibility to give your child some wiggle room. If everything is nonnegotiable, then everything is tempting to the child who tends to break boundaries; if she has flexible options, she's more likely to be reasonable.

If you restrict your child's options and everything outside of your ideal neat-as-a-pin bedroom is a firm no-no, when she decides to push the limits she'll go all out: perishable food squirreled away, floor buried under layers of debris, permanent damage to furniture or walls. However, if you're willing to be flexible on certain aspects, she'll be able to experiment in a more controlled manner.

You'll need to reevaluate and adjust each of these lines and areas as necessary. There is no one-size-fits-all model; every family has different values, different norms, and even different definitions of safety.

And remember: just because it's in the area of flexibility doesn't mean you have to be flexible in every particular case! Many children can be expected to follow the limits that you set; if it's in the area of flexibility, you *can* be flexible at times—but you don't *have* to always be flexible. Picture the tree bending in the storm: when there's no wind, there's no need to bend; in the face of conflict or struggle, flexibility may be necessary and effective.

Think about it: you may not allow your children anywhere near the stove until they're practically adults, while your professional-chef neighbor teaches her three-year-old to cook. You may allow boy/girl sleepovers in your home, while your religious friend minimizes play dates and contact with children of the opposite sex.

Of course, you're not going to start diagramming and launching into long-winded explanations about values every time your child wants to change up the schedule a bit. When an opportunity to be flexible arises, it doesn't warrant major effort or lecturing; keep it simple with these guidelines:

- Observe (like the mindfulness skills): Take a step back from the situation and notice what's going on with your child. Is she excited? Has he been having a hard time? Has she been behaving poorly?

- Ask your child to explain his perspective: What is he feeling? Why does he want this?

- Actively listen and reflect: "So you're telling me that this is the must-see movie and you really want to see it with your friends, is that right?" [Extra points for validation!]

- Do your homework: Sometimes "everyone" really is going to be there or has the newest fad, in which case it may be important for you to be flexible.

- Express your willingness to be flexible: Show your child that you're willing to work with him.

- Establish limits: These can be either existing limits or new limits, depending on the situation.

- Follow through: Maintain the new or existing limits.

Congratulations! You've learned how to strike the consistency/flexibility (and acceptance/change) balance.

Consistency and Flexibility in Action

Eleven-year-old Elise has a session with a math tutor every Wednesday at 6:00. It's Wednesday afternoon and the weather is beautiful; Elise's friends are riding their bikes to the ice cream store and then hanging out at the park. She wants to go along and asks you to cancel the tutor.

Dad: Elise, you know that you need your tutor, especially now that the year is almost over. You have a final coming up, and I want you to be prepared, so I need to say no to going out with your friends today.

Elise:	But Dad, everyone is going! I'm going to miss the best day ever! Don't you want me to have friends? I have to go out if I want to be part of a good group.
Dad:	*(noticing that Elise is getting worked up about this and knowing that Elise has been struggling socially)* I can see that this is really important to you. We've talked about this before—you know that you need the tutoring session. I'm not sure why you're feeling so upset. Can you help me understand?
Elise:	Yes! I finally found a group of friends that I really like, and if I don't hang out with them, they might dump me and find someone else. Besides, I never cancel the tutor!
Dad:	That's true, you are always very responsible about your tutoring and you really want a break now. I understand. And I can see that all of your friends are already waiting across the street. Tell you what. We'll cancel the tutor for today, but I want to make it very clear that we are not going to cancel again—you will need to continue with your tutor every Wednesday until summer vacation, which means another five sessions. Do you understand?
Elise:	Yes, totally, I won't cancel again. Thanks, Dad, you're the best!

Fast forward three weeks. The weather is perfect and the gang is rollerblading at the beach. (Why do they always pick Wednesdays for fun activities?!) Elise approaches Dad again.

Elise:	*(wheedling)* Dad, I really want to go rollerblading today, it's an awesome beach day! Can I skip the tutor today? I think I really know the math well.
Dad:	Elise, remember our conversation last time? No canceling. You agreed that you'd work with the tutor every Wednesday until the end of the year. I'm sorry, you need to meet with your tutor today. You can rollerblade up and down the block until your tutor gets here.

*[Dad even managed to work in some flexibility and valida-
tion there!]*

Elise: But Dad, it's not fair! They're totally going to dump me! I
have to be there! And I know the stupid math! Please?
Rollerblading on the block isn't even in the same league
as blading at the beach.

Dad: No, Elise, that was our agreement. You can't cancel the
tutor today.

Elise: *(storms off to tell her friends about the meanest dad in the
universe)*

Now, because the world works in strange ways, Elise's tutor calls shortly
thereafter to cancel the session; Elise rushes to catch up with her friends. Even
though she wound up missing the session, she still learned that her dad is
serious about enforcing his limits—*and* that he can be flexible, too.

Remember this: being flexible does not mean allowing your child to wear
you down. Make your decision based on the circumstances, then follow the
guidelines for balancing consistency with flexibility.

Let's look at another scenario:

Noah comes home from day camp with a special prize: a twenty-ounce
bottle of soda (who comes up with these prizes?). The house rule is "no soda on
weekdays"—and Noah is well aware of that rule. That doesn't stop him from
pleading his case.

Noah: Dad! Dad! Look what I got for a prize today!

Dad: Wow, son, that's a great prize! Let's put it away for
Saturday.

Noah: But Daaad, I want to drink some now! It's so hot outside,
and I'm so thirsty, and it was a special prize!

Dad: Noah, you know the rule. No soda on weekdays.

Noah: C'mon, Dad, you never let me have any. This was special!
I could have had it in camp and you never would have
known! At least I brought it home to show it to you! Next
time I'll just drink it and you won't know the difference.

Dad: Okay. Fine. Just don't tell Mom, and don't let the other kids see it.

Noah got what he wanted...without learning that consistency is important. The next time he wants to bend a rule, he'll know exactly which parent to appeal to. Plus, Dad immediately reinforced Noah's complaining and arguing, which means that Noah will almost certainly repeat the behavior—even more strongly—at the next opportunity.

It's okay for Dad to be flexible and let Noah drink his soda, but there's a more effective way to go about it.

Noah: Dad! Dad! Look what I got for a prize today!

Dad: Wow, son, that's a great prize! Let's put it away for Saturday.

Noah: But Daaad, I want to drink some now! It's so hot outside, and I'm so thirsty, and it was a special prize!

Dad: Hmm, I can see that you worked hard to earn that! You know what, today I'm going to make an exception because I'm so proud of the effort that you put in. You can have it now, but remember, this is a special exception and the rule still remains. Got it?

Noah: Got it!

Because this is a realistic scenario, thirty seconds later Dad is accosted by Mason, Noah's brother.

Mason: Dad, it's not fair! Why did Noah get soda? You never let us have soda on weekdays! I want soda too!

Dad: Mason, sometimes things don't seem exactly fair, and I made an exception in this case.

[*Dad repeats his response as necessary or moves onto planned ignoring ("Mason, I am not going to discuss this further.")*]

Dad has just (admirably) managed to be consistent with one child and flexible with another at the same time, considering each child's present needs and the situation at hand.

It's okay if your other kids are jealous of the flexibility that you're showing their sibling (as long as you make exceptions in roughly equal measure for all of them). You can't—and shouldn't—protect your children from every emotion. It's okay to have emotions; if children aren't expected to deal with their emotions, they cannot learn to self-soothe and self-regulate when their lives don't go as planned. Go ahead and help your child regulate his emotions (validation skills will come in handy here)—without giving in.

Explain clearly and calmly why their sibling got something that he didn't (briefly and when appropriate); don't expect your child to magically understand and be happy (after all, he probably doesn't really care about the explanation— he cares that he didn't get any soda!). You can also turn the situation into a teaching moment for the child who benefited from the flexibility: "Noah, please don't flaunt the soda in front of your brother; be sensitive to his feelings."

Roadblocks to Limit Setting

The road to limit setting isn't always a smooth one; several common obstacles may stand in the way of your effectiveness. If you're having difficulty implementing limits, you'll probably identify with one or several of these roadblocks:

- **Emotions:** Our emotions often stand in the way of effective limit setting, for example, fear ("He's going to blow up about this, and then who knows what he'll do?"), guilt ("Look at his poor, sad little face; maybe he's right and I'm being really mean"), and helplessness or hopelessness ("I give up—he's never going to respond to this" or "I have no control over this child").

- **Lack of skill:** Now that you're armed with the limit-setting skills in this chapter, you have the skills you need to assist you!

- **Lack of confidence:** This is one of those times in your life when it's better to fake it till you make it; even if you don't feel confident, try to appear confident.

- **Indecisiveness:** "I can't decide if this is the right thing to do." That's where your skills and the Model of Flexibility come in. Also, keep in mind that it's okay to not know the "right" answer—sometimes you'll need to take risks in order to learn what's most effective.

- **Negative childhood experiences:** "My parents never let me do anything, so I went totally crazy and did stupid things once I was out of the house—I don't want to be anything like them." There's no need to overcompensate or swing to the other extreme; you *can* say "no" and set limits without smothering your child.

- **Insufficient time or patience:** Once you've practiced effective limit setting a few times, it gets easier and doesn't always require a lot of time (plus, as time goes on, it'll require less time and energy as you develop confidence in your skills). Use mindfulness skills to increase your patience, and be realistic about the fact that limit setting can really test your patience!

- **Stress or negative headspace:** Again, use mindfulness skills to get into the right frame of mind before setting limits; if you're not regulated enough to set limits, wait until you're calmer—even if it means missing an opportunity to set a limit.

One major roadblock to effective limit setting is unhelpful assumptions and beliefs (AKA myths). Identify and counteract these myths before (and during) limit setting to reassure yourself that you're doing the right thing for your child, your family, and yourself. Let's take a look at some common beliefs. (You can also find the Chapter 8 Roadblock Cards, with some additional beliefs and helpful responses, at http://www.newharbinger.com/46868.)

Belief: *My child will hate me for this!*

Au contraire! While your child may fight the limits you set, having limits increases your child's level of security and feeling of being cared for. Even if it doesn't seem like it in the heat of the moment (and chances are it won't), limits help your child feel and know that she is loved. (Don't worry—even if she doesn't express it, she'll understand it better as she gets older and realizes that you just want her to be safe, successful, and healthy.)

A fascinating example: I once worked with a mother of a challenging ten-year-old daughter who constantly fought the limits her parents imposed. The girl had to fill out a form for a school Mother's Day project. One section read, "I know my mother loves me because…" and this girl—who constantly fought her mother's every attempt at limit setting—wrote, "she makes rules and bedtime."

Belief: *If I always say yes and am consistently positive, she'll be so confident that she'll learn to create and enforce her own limits!*

It's a nice thought, but untrue. Children have parents for a reason; they will not "just figure it out" on their own and become self-regulating adults. Children are developmentally unable to limit themselves or understand intuitively what is right and what is wrong.

If a parent never tells his child no, the child will be unable to say no to himself, leading to behaviors with long-term damaging effects. Children need to be taught to harness their urges and control themselves—it's generally not an inborn ability.

Research shows that children raised without limits lack the ability to develop self-discipline and exhibit increased impulsivity. As we discussed in chapter 7, avoiding discipline and limit setting (in other words, permissive parenting) often results in children who have difficulty with self-regulation (Baumrind 1967; Jabeen and Anis-ul-Haque 2013; Alizadeh et al. 2011).

Struggles in childhood help the child build resilience and prepare for the challenges of life. A parent who attempts to shield his child from normal childhood difficulties and disappointments effectively hampers the child's ability to handle life's greater difficulties.

Imagine this: a man comes across a butterfly attempting to exit the chrysalis. He observes the butterfly's struggles; it seems to be in pain and the process is arduous. Taking pity on the butterfly, he takes a pair of scissors and frees the creature. However, the butterfly is shriveled and underdeveloped; it depends on the natural exit from the chrysalis to form fully.

Children are like that butterfly. As much as it pains you to see your child struggle, overcoming challenges is necessary to help him become an adult who can handle life's bumpy road.

When a parent sets limits effectively, she considers the parent-child relationship, so she is secure in the knowledge that her child is receiving a well-balanced outpouring of love and affection.

Belief: *Limits are controlling and punitive.*

When it's done effectively, within reason, and with the proper considerations taken, setting limits is not controlling or punitive. If it's controlling or punitive, it's not being executed effectively—it's most likely based on emotions and impulsivity rather than mindfulness.

Children crave and thrive on structure and predictability. They also want and need to see their parents' strength and confidence; it increases their sense of security. If a child sees that her parent is easily swayed or vulnerable, her trust and confidence in her parent is compromised.

Belief: *I can't do this!*

Yes, you can! It's difficult—and you can do it. Believing that you can't do it will interfere with your effectiveness. It's okay if your child is disappointed, sad, or upset; your child has emotions, and that's normal and healthy. It does get easier with time and consistency; as long as you don't give in to (and reinforce) tantrums and arguments, they will eventually decrease. Give it time and don't give up!

We're people—not machines. We're inherently unable to perform with perfect precision every time. Don't expect to strike the consistency/flexibility balance every time. The goal isn't to *always* get it right; the goal is to do the best you can. At the end of a tough day, you're likely to be less skillful. You may find yourself analyzing your parenting and realizing in hindsight that you were too strict or too flexible.

Don't get stuck on those single encounters. Look at the bigger picture rather than the day-to-day: *Am I effectively balancing consistency and flexibility overall?* If the answer is yes, then the small slipups won't ruin the balance in the long run. If the answer is no, remember that you're doing the best you can.

You'll use your limit-setting skills, along with all your other acceptance and change skills, to effectively parent your child. While this concludes our skill-based chapters (congratulations for reading it through!), chapter 9 will help you balance various factors within and outside of your family and put all of these skills into practice.

Finding Your Family's Balance

You've made it through the book! You're now armed with an incredible assortment of skills, knowledge, and understanding that will help you climb your parenthood mountain. Kudos to you for embarking on this vital journey! It will inevitably be a bumpy ride, and now you're equipped with the tools and knowledge to navigate the challenges along the way.

It can be truly empowering to start getting your parenting under control.

Often, though, you can run into some pretty significant roadblocks along the way, some of which you may have already experienced over the course of reading this book.

Even when you're fully committed to implementing everything you've learned, you and your child do not exist in a vacuum. There are numerous factors—both human and environmental—that can potentially interfere with your effectiveness.

Maybe you'll meet resistance from your co-parent (whether you're raising your child together or separately). He or she may be unwilling to get on board or refuse to cooperate, derailing your efforts. "My parents didn't do any of this stuff and I turned out just fine." "There's nothing wrong with this kid, he just needs to grow up a little." "I can't deal with this anymore; he's all yours!" Or your child's other parent may interact with the child in a way that impedes your effectiveness. "Dad said I'll always be a loser, no matter what." "Well, Mom said I don't have to be back on time!" "I don't care about that stupid chart; Dad will let me buy whichever sneakers I want anyway."

Sometimes, it's balancing the needs and safety of your other children with parenting an uncontrollable child that can be an overwhelming struggle. You may need to protect your children from their sibling's rages. You may need to juggle validating siblings without judging the uncontrollable child. You may need to deal with children who feel slighted or overlooked or who complain about unfair dynamics. "He's crazy!" "Why does she always get away with everything?" "He's ruining my life! I can't stand this!" "You're always driving her to appointments and spending special time with her and you can't even buy me new school supplies." "Why are you picking on me for not making my bed when his room looks like a tornado hit it?"

You may face obstacles in the form of grandparents, friends, teachers, or environmental factors. For example, you may be working extremely hard on validation and acceptance, only to discover that your child's super-critical teacher destroys your efforts. Or you may think it would be so good for her to have her own room, but you simply don't have the space. Or Grandma might openly disapprove of your parenting in front of the kids: "How could you let them get away with that?"

And here you thought the biggest hurdle would be the uncontrollable child herself!

As much as we'd love to have an ideal situation where everyone cooperates, that's very rarely the reality. You can use all of your acceptance and change skills to address the complexities of your family's dynamics.

When working with another adult (e.g., spouse, partner, co-parent, grandparent), communication is essential. Find out why she doesn't want to cooperate (look for causes). Take time to talk to your spouse (partner, co-parent, grandparent, or other adult); discuss why you want to try these techniques and how she can make a difference. If she resists, suggest a trial period to see what happens—"Let's try this for a week; there's nothing to lose!" You can try the same tactic in a school setting by talking with your child's teacher: advocate for your child and share what's worked for you at home.

If your spouse, or the other adult, has a hard time with a specific strategy or set of skills, try to balance your roles. For example, if he constantly loses his cool when trying to set limits or give consequences, try taking over the discipline for a while as he focuses on positivity and acceptance.

If he simply won't get on board, practice acceptance. Let go of blame and try to find the kernel of truth in his viewpoint. Even if you feel like you're swimming against the tide, don't give up! Every small step that you take can make a difference.

Validation is important when dealing with your other children as well. Life is hard with an uncontrollable sibling, and validating that can go a long way. "Yes, it's scary when he gets so mad at you. I know it's hard for you. You can always come and tell me how you feel. I'm so proud of you for trying so hard to get along with everyone, even if I don't always tell you that. We all have our struggles; you also have things you need to work on. He's still your brother, and he does really fun things with you too, like giving you rides and building cool LEGO cities."

When you have an uncontrollable child as well as a child or children whose behavior is easier to manage, it can be easy to overlook the non-squeaky wheel. He's not demanding your attention or your resources; she's doing fine in school; they don't melt down when you buy the wrong cereal...so it may be hard to remember that they have needs, too. Be mindful of all of your children's needs: protect them from their sibling's severe behavior (without judgment), make special time for them, praise them, reward them. Don't wait for them to come complain or to start acting up for some of your attention. Take proactive action—even in simple gestures or words—to satiate their need for your love, approval, and attention.

Every family has its own complex dynamics, and we couldn't possibly address all of the potential issues here. If you need more help balancing your family's particular needs, you may want to consider family therapy. This gives your family a safe environment in which to work as a unit to tackle your challenges.

Maintaining your equilibrium while parenting your children can be tough. Stay strong! Even when the challenges seem insurmountable, remember: change is constant. Ride out those changes within your family dynamic as you balance acceptance with change.

Balance in Action

Remember Lily and Tyler from chapter 1? Take a look at their families to see how they've found their balance.

Both sets of parents report that their children are now perfect angels who never misbehave and who have apologized profusely and repeatedly for their former behavior.

(Now, wouldn't that be nice?)

Here's how they *really* fared.

After several months of learning, implementing, practicing, fine-tuning, and evaluating their skills, Lily's and Tyler's parents describe significant improvements in the atmosphere at home and in their relationships with their children.

Lily's Story (as Told by Her Parents)

When we started reading through the acceptance chapters, we figured that we'd be able to read through them quickly and get right to change. We accepted our sweet little girl, even with her faults, and were eager to start changing Lily's behavior.

We cruised right through the first set of acceptance strategies, mentally checking off most of the skills (and patting ourselves on the back). Some of them, like willing hands and opposite action, were helpful when dealing with Lily's outbursts.

Chapter 4—mindfulness—was when we realized that we may not have been as accepting as we'd thought. We had labeled Lily as "too sensitive," and that was something that bothered us. We discovered that we'd been judging Lily's sensitivity as a bad thing (which is natural, as it was really affecting our household).

To remedy that issue, we took a long, hard look at the causes of Lily's behavior. Some of them are "nature" based: Lily had been a colicky baby and hard-to-soothe toddler, and Dad's family tends to be more sensitive. Other causes are rooted in "nurture," influenced by her environment: Lily had some trouble acclimating to school, she was teased for her social anxiety in the early years, her sister poked fun at her for being a "crybaby," and we've pressured Lily to try new things when she's anxious. It makes sense that she's sensitive!

With a lot of practice, we learned to replace our exasperated "She's so sensitive" with a less judgmental "Lily's sensitive" observation. Even though it's still hard and often painful to deal with Lily's sensitivity, we know that this is the way she "should" be. We've worked hard to start loving and appreciating all of Lily—not only when she's cute and giggly and precocious, but also when she's being "too" sensitive.

Then we promptly returned to the acceptance skills and reread them with our new nonjudgmental bias. The pros and cons skill helped us see the positive attributes of Lily's sensitivity. She can't handle it when other people are upset, and she often gets upset as a result. While that's unpleasant, there's a positive side: she's sensitive to others' feelings and is kind to her friends, lets her sister play with her toys, and will run to comfort her crying toddler brother (though she gets upset when he doesn't stop).

Next was validation, which was a game-changer for us—and for Lily.

We'd always tried validating Lily's feelings; however, we'd been doing it wrong. (Okay, ineffectively.) We had done a lot of "I understand that you're upset, but it's really not that big a deal" or "Yes, it's very sad that your toy broke, but it's time to move on."

We also did plenty of invalidating and attempting to reason with Lily when she got upset, especially on those days when we did everything "right" and she still melted down. "We went online three times to find the perfect prize and now you're throwing a tantrum because it's not exactly the right color—enough is enough!"

Through validation, we learned how to find out what's hurting Lily and make sense of it. We've learned to communicate our understanding without catering to her whims.

Of course, it's not a fail-safe technique. Sometimes even the most textbook-worthy validation doesn't work with Lily, and too much validation backfires as well. She'll get more worked up and carry on: "Okay, so if you get it, just let me do it!" "If you understand, then why don't you just punish her?" "If that would make you mad too, you should call the teacher and yell at her!"

Attempting to reason with her just results in power struggles. When we see that validating isn't effective, we move onto a change skill, usually extinction (planned ignoring). Extinction is also our go-to when Lily tells us that she hates us or wishes we'd die—we will not validate or reinforce that.

In the beginning, we'd punish her for saying hurtful things to us or for screaming or pinching herself. We sent her to her room, but she'd just escalate when we did that. We realized that these consequences made Lily feel like there was something wrong with her and that her sensitivity was a bad attribute. She'd scream and cry; sometimes she'd give us insight into her mind with comments like "I always have to go to my room because I cry too much and get upset. I'm a bad girl."

Lily's outbursts also resulted in a lot of negative attention: she'd say hurtful or shocking things and get a reaction. All that attention was reinforcing her behavior and encouraging her to repeat it. We turned to extinction, with the predictable behavioral burst, but eventually she realized that she wasn't going to get a reaction out of us. Extinction works well for her, as long as she isn't hurting anyone else (which happens on rare occasions).

When Lily reacts extra-strongly to extinction or takes a long time to cool down, we do occasionally take her up to her room to deescalate. When we do, we explicitly tell her that it's not a punishment—so that she doesn't feel rejected—and that she can come out as soon as she feels calmer. Her siblings deserve to live in a home not ruled by chaos!

To help Lily manage her overwhelming emotions, we encouraged her to make a "calm box" to keep in her room. With our help, she filled a shoebox with a stress ball, Silly Putty, a coloring book, and a preloaded iPod for her to use when she needs to calm down.

Validation has made a big difference in the way our family runs. We've stopped walking on eggshells to avoid setting Lily off. Instead, we help her handle triggering situations head-on. We know that she's still likely to melt down, but now that we have the confidence and skills to deal with it—and the knowledge that we're doing the right thing—we're able to weather the storm.

After a while, we noticed that all of our reflecting Lily's feelings and empathizing with her was starting to take effect. Naming her emotions and teaching her to name them really helps her self-regulate. Heartened by her progress, we made sure to praise her effusively and constantly, pointing out when she handled disappointments and anger like a big girl. We even threw in some small rewards on occasion (as intermittent reinforcement) to strengthen her behavior, accompanied by more praise: "Lily, we're so proud of the way you controlled yourself just now. That kind of behavior deserves a special treat!"

While she still tantrums more than the "average" kid her age, her outbursts have noticeably decreased in frequency and length. However, as time went on, we realized that she'd still revert to verbal assaults when she was out of sorts. We decided to pay closer attention to reducing those assaults because they were (and are) the most hurtful to us and to her siblings.

We sat Lily down and told her how proud we were of her for coming so far. We told her, "We understand that it can be hard not to say hurtful things when we're angry, so we'd like to reward you for not saying mean things to other people or hurting their feelings."

That appealed to her sensitive side—she doesn't want to hurt other people, but sometimes it slips out when she's upset. We told her that she'd earn tokens for using specific skills (with one prompt) when she's angry rather than taking it out on others: going to her room, using her "calm box," playing with her stuffed animals, working on an art project, and telling the other person why she's upset without hurtful language.

Together, we made up a list of things that she'd be able to "buy" with her tokens. We had to veto some of the more outlandish suggestions (including a pet pony and a trip to Disneyland) before settling on a list of "big" prizes (long term) and "small" prizes (short term).

We fashioned a "token jar" by cutting a slit in the lid of an empty pickle jar and letting Lily decorate it. The token jar now sits in her room so that she automatically gets some breathing room whenever she earns a token.

So far, she's earned enough tokens to get a first-tier prize (an ice cream sundae) and is halfway to her second prize! We make sure to include lots of praise, too, to develop Lily's intrinsic motivation. Every time Lily uses her skills to calm down and regulate, we applaud her self-control and inner strength.

We know that consistency is important, especially for kids like Lily. We also know that flexibility is important, sometimes even more than consistency. So there are times when we let the behavior slide, pretend not to notice, or let her off with a warning. This has caught her sister's attention, who complains that it's not fair, so we've had to have the "fair doesn't mean equal" discussion with her several times—while validating her feelings, too. To head off further jealousy, we created a chart for her, and she's happily earning a prize for keeping her room clean. Win-win!

Overall, our lives are definitely calmer, our home more pleasant. Lily's teachers say that she's become more assertive in school when someone bothers her. We've even managed to reclaim date night as Lily's behavior has improved!

Most importantly, Lily is happier. She's become a lot more expressive and open about her feelings now that she's not feeling invalidated, judged, or labeled. Our smiley, giggly Lily surfaces more frequently than the Mr. Hyde-esque version, and we treasure every happy, cuddly, joyful moment.

There's still work to do—and we know that we can do it!

Tyler's Story

Parenting Tyler has been a bumpy journey from the start.

Since preschool, Tyler's given us a run for our money. The first several years of school were excruciating as he turned our home and his school upside down and inside out. We searched for answers as his school threatened expulsion for fighting, out-of-control behavior, classroom misconduct, and a total lack of respect for authority. He had few friends and we were constantly frazzled, especially when he turned on his defenseless baby brother, Alex.

We dragged Tyler to several therapists, psychologists, and psychiatrists, looking for answers. His ADHD diagnosis came pretty quickly; we recognized it early on and explored different options with varying degrees of success. We changed his diet, gave him supplements, researched every type of therapy and tried dozens.

When we started Tyler on medication (a journey in its own right, until we finally found the appropriate medication and dosage), the school-related stresses finally abated. We started hearing positive reports from his teachers for the very first time. He started bringing home decent grades. We cried the first time a classmate called to invite him to a birthday party.

While we should have been celebrating, we were too worn out, too jaded, too wary to enjoy the reprieve. Parenting Tyler depleted all of our natural optimism and strength, leaving us unsure of our own capabilities and unable to connect with him in a meaningful way. After so many years of negativity and power struggles, our relationship was virtually nonexistent.

It didn't help that our home life was only marginally better. Sometimes it seemed that the medication actually made it worse, especially during that crazy time of day when it starts wearing off.

Recently, Tyler's psychiatrist suggested, based on his history, that he may have disruptive mood dysregulation disorder, or DMDD. We'd never heard of it. She described the symptoms of the disorder, and it definitely fit Tyler. Because he's already doing well on medication and in therapy, she explained that his course of treatment wouldn't change much. She did, however, recommend finding a DBT therapist for Tyler and for parent training. We balked; another type of therapy? We'd been through so many that we were skeptical, but guardedly willing to give it a try.

Acceptance felt like an insurmountable mountain. While we were able to list his redeeming qualities—his sense of humor, his handiness—it felt detached, like we were describing someone else's child. And those good qualities were always linked to negative things: "He's lucky he's funny, it helps him get away with murder. "He'd better put those skills to good use to fix all of the things he's broken in this house."

It was so hard to accept Tyler. So hard to make peace with the fact that he isn't like other kids his age. So hard to acknowledge that he "shouldn't" be acting like everyone else. And so hard to recognize that we are not total failures as parents.

Slowly, painfully, we came to realize that Tyler felt the negativity. He felt like the no-good one, the rotten apple, the bad seed, especially next to Alex, who has typical childhood struggles. It was impacting our relationship, impacting his self-esteem, impacting his ability to behave appropriately.

We had to do a lot of retraining our brains and repairing our relationship before we were able to even start thinking about change.

We started with ourselves, working on straight-up acceptance. We did it all. We crept into Tyler's room at night to look at him (and stopped that after the night that he woke up and freaked out to catch us staring at him "like weirdos"). We made endless lists of his good qualities (sadly, in the beginning, we sat for hours with almost-blank pages). We tried to find any shred of similarity between him and us ("when I was a teen, I also gave my parents a run for their money!"). We came up with all sorts of mantras, some more helpful than others; we practiced opposite action, which calmed us down but invoked Tyler's suspicions (he didn't say anything, but he definitely eyed us mistrustfully).

Mindfulness taught us that our assumptions about Tyler were sometimes unfounded, even though they were often spot-on. Because he caused chaos in our home for so long, it became natural for us to jump to conclusions. We've learned that we don't always know what he's thinking. And we've learned to separate our thoughts from our emotions (we're still working on that one).

When we started validating Tyler, he was mistrustful (plenty of "Why are you guys acting so weird these days?"). He was cynical, almost like he was waiting for the other shoe to drop, and that was heartbreaking for us—it made us realize just how little validation we'd given him until now.

Slowly, so slowly, he started warming up. We began to feel emotions other than exasperation and pain with Tyler. We loosened up a bit, became more affectionate and tolerant, and Tyler started responding in kind. (Somewhat.) We listened to his feedback and reactions, learning which statements were effective and validating and which felt condescending to him.

Validating ourselves was tough too, especially because of Mom's work with kids. Mom constantly doubted her abilities and felt like a hypocrite— after all, if she couldn't parent our own kid, how could she possibly work with other people's kids?

After a while of focusing on acceptance (and impatiently holding off on change), we decided to introduce some change strategies. We sat down and listed the behaviors that we were most desperate to change, then prioritized them. Physical aggression came first, because that is unacceptable in our books and there have been times that we were genuinely afraid someone would get seriously hurt.

Before talking to Tyler, we held a "cope-ahead session" to figure out the best way to go about it. Based on Tyler's reactions to these conversations in the past, we were fairly sure we knew how he'd respond. We planned the discussion, prepared some phrases and skills that we'd probably need to use, and even practiced on each other, even though it was awkward!

We called Tyler in for a meeting and clearly laid out the rules of physical aggression. We factually (mindfully and nonjudgmentally) described the behaviors that needed to change: punching, hitting, shoving, and spitting. From now on, we said, those behaviors would result in an immediate loss of privileges (screen time, special outings with Dad, staying out with friends) for twenty-four hours.

Predictably, there was a defensive uproar from Tyler, but we followed the guidelines: we were calm, focused, and firm.

Those first few weeks were tough, to put it mildly. It seemed that Tyler took every opportunity to test his limits. When Tyler started flicking Alex, he protested that "flicking wasn't part of the agreement." He'd insist that he "had" to push Alex for making faces at him. He bellowed that we weren't punishing Alex for knocking Tyler's papers off of the table, so he took care of it and punched him.

Tyler lost plenty of privileges and it seemed like the situation was deteriorating rather than improving. Our therapist assured us that Tyler's behaviors may get worse before they get better, and that it was hopefully a sign of better times to come. She encouraged us to keep track of his outbursts to make sure our expectations weren't unreasonable.

She also pointed out that we were focusing on the punitive, negative aspect, and suggested that we introduce incentives for good behavior.

With that advice, we sat down with Tyler again. We told him that we saw how hard it is for him to not hurt Alex and wanted to offer him a reward for improved behavior. On days that he's not aggressive between the hours of 4:30 and 7:00 (his peak aggression time), he gets an extra dollar toward his allowance. At the same time, we continue to enforce the loss of privileges on days that he is aggressive.

We almost threw in the towel many times, but we worked hard to be as consistent as possible. We adopted a few "consequence mantras": Don't engage. Don't threaten. Just let the consequence do the work. The planned ignoring and broken record skills were sanity saving during the initial adjustment period.

In the past, these encounters would escalate, with Tyler spiraling out of control and us heaping more punishments on him for every infraction. Now, we stick with the agreed-upon consequences and are grateful to have a framework to guide our reactions.

There is rarely room for flexibility when it comes to physical harm. Once in a while, we find an opportunity to be flexible with Tyler. There was the time that Tyler had a few great days in a row, then started to fight with Alex but stopped immediately when prompted. We praised his self-control and let that "almost-punch" incident slide.

Thankfully, natural consequences have come along too, and we've used them to our advantage. One day, Tyler had been taunting Alex mercilessly all afternoon. He'd also touched Alex hard enough to bother him but not hard enough to be considered "aggressive": giving him noogies, slapping him five just a tad too hard, "accidentally" tripping him.

Later in the day, Tyler tried to sweet-talk Alex into letting him use his new scooter. After a long afternoon of subtle torment, though, Alex had no intention of sharing. When Tyler appealed to us for help, we calmly told him that we understood why Alex wouldn't want to share. He definitely got the message (even though he exploded that nobody understands him and that "it wouldn't kill Alex to be nice once in a while").

Throughout it all, we monitored the effectiveness of our efforts and noticed that the aggression was actually decreasing! Because we paid attention and kept a log, we were able to celebrate this victory instead of focusing on the fact that he was still hurting his brother with relative frequency.

In addition to the physical aggression issue, we realized that we had difficulty setting and enforcing limits with Tyler. He was consistently breaking curfew, strolling in at the end of dinnertime, and refusing to do his homework or clean up after himself. He also became a master at playing us against each other, getting one of us to agree to something and defying the other. It felt like Tyler was running the house, not us!

Once we'd begun strengthening our relationship and growing a backbone, we decided to tackle limit setting and being consistent. A lot of the issues that we dealt with—mostly by ineffectually threatening, *grounding, and punishing—could have been avoided had we put the right limits in place.*

We started tackling the limits one by one, beginning with Tyler's noncompliance with turning off his video games. He'd simply refuse to turn off his game when we told him to, despite plenty of screaming on our part, which led to frustration, resentment, anger, and hurt feelings on all sides.

We agreed on a limit and introduced it: Tyler gets a five-minute warning and then has to turn off the game as soon as he's told. If he doesn't comply, he loses five minutes from his next game.

He tested that limit immediately. He simply refused to turn off the game, and the next day—when he was supposed to turn it off five minutes earlier—he shrugged his shoulders and said, "Make me."

How exactly do you "make" a thirteen-year-old who's bigger than you turn off his game?

You unplug it, of course, and take the power cord. Drama-free.

There was plenty of drama from Tyler, though.

He became belligerent. Furious. Out of control. We practiced our extinction skills, ignoring his temper tantrum. We left the house with Alex while Tyler raged. When we came back, all we got was a sneer and a "Ha ha, you left the house, that's exactly what I wanted. Peace and quiet." We sacrificed one skill—reinforcing his behavior by letting him feel, in some way, that he'd "won"—in order to achieve consistency and effective extinction.

The whole encounter left us shaken and upset, and also proud of ourselves for weathering the storm.

When the drama died down, we reexamined our strategy. Apparently, losing five minutes wasn't working for Tyler (and neither was repeatedly yelling at him to turn off the game, like we'd done before setting this limit). On the other hand, taking away the power cord sure was effective. We switched tacks to enforce the limit: if you don't turn it off when we tell you to (after the five-minute warning), the cord is ours for the next day.

Tyler grumbled about how we don't trust him and how we treat him like a baby; we matter-of-factly ended the discussion and ignored all further comments. The next time he took his time turning off his game, the cord disappeared for a day. He's become remarkably compliant since then!

It takes a lot of mindful self-control to keep our anger in check when enforcing these limits. We've found ourselves helplessly threatening that we'd ground him for two weeks or not let him go on errands ever again. Our emotions run high, especially when Tyler reacts strongly, and sometimes we give in to those emotions against our better judgment.

We try hard to take space and regulate ourselves when dealing with Tyler's limit breaking, but sometimes we don't have the presence of mind (or, as busy parents, the physical ability) to do it. It's easier when we are both there together, because one of us can take a break while the other holds down the fort. There's a pretty steep learning curve, and we're still learning every day, but practice has made it better.

There are still plenty of bumps in our lives. Parenting Tyler will never be the "easy" journey that it is for some parents. With our new skills, though, we feel more confident, and we've seen real progress. There's been a marked decline in uncontrollable behaviors and noticeable improvements in Tyler's mood, our moods, and our relationship. We feel empowered—and heartened by the very real improvements that we've seen—to continue loving both of our sons through the ups and downs of life.

Know Before You Go

Just as a car requires regular maintenance and checkups to run smoothly and continuously, parenting requires far more than a one-time tune-up. Constant and consistent self-evaluation and ongoing support are two of the keys to successful parenting.

Now that you've learned so many skills and concepts, it can be hard to remember all of the nuances and details! This Parenting Skills Master Checklist, also available to download at http://www.newharbinger.com/46868, serves as a summary and quick reference guide to help you through your everyday parenting moments. Use it whenever you need a reminder or when you evaluate your skill use for maximum effectiveness.

PARENTING SKILLS MASTER CHECKLIST

Dialectical Skills **(Chapter 1)**

- ☐ Use dialectical language (*both, and, effective, often, sometimes* as opposed to *but, always, never, right, wrong, good, bad*).
- ☐ Look for, honor, and validate the truth on the other side.
- ☐ Work to embrace change without fighting it.
- ☐ Practice accepting change.
- ☐ Pay attention to your effect on others.
- ☐ Look for causes without blaming or judging.

Remind Yourself of the Benefits of Acceptance **(Chapter 2)**

- ☐ Pain + acceptance = pain; pain + nonacceptance = suffering.
- ☐ Acceptance leads to change (fighting reality impedes change).
- ☐ Acceptance increases the ability to cope.
- ☐ Acceptance improves relationships in the long term.

Acceptance Skills **(Chapter 3)**

- ☐ Identify and weigh the pros and cons of acceptance versus nonacceptance.
- ☐ Connect with the child by listing his attributes and looking for similarities.
- ☐ Turn your mind toward acceptance.
- ☐ Practice half smile and willing hands when feeling willful.
- ☐ Practice opposite action.
- ☐ Cope ahead.
- ☐ Radically accept reality:
  - ☐ Observe yourself: are you accepting or fighting reality?
  - ☐ Look at causes.
  - ☐ Let go of blame.
  - ☐ Make meaning.
  - ☐ Embrace change.
  - ☐ Let your emotions arise; notice the sadness and other feelings.

Mindfulness Skills (Chapter 4)

- ☐ Use "what" skills:
  - ☐ Observe
  - ☐ Describe
  - ☐ Participate
- ☐ Use "how" skills:
  - ☐ Nonjudgmentally
  - ☐ One-mindfully
  - ☐ Effectively

Validation Skills (Chapter 5)

- ☐ Use verbal and/or functional validation to make your child feel understood.
- ☐ Validate the valid, not the invalid; find the kernel of truth. You don't have to agree or approve.
- ☐ Practice the six levels of validation:
  - ☐ Be present.
  - ☐ Reflect without judgment.
  - ☐ Look for clues about the child's feelings and try to name his emotion.
  - ☐ Communicate understanding based on the past.
  - ☐ Validate based on the present.
  - ☐ Validate genuinely.
- ☐ Ask the child for help and insight when you don't understand.
- ☐ Gently provide invalidation when it's necessary and constructive.
- ☐ Evaluate effectiveness; if validation isn't working, try something else.

Strategies to Increase Behavior (Chapter 6)

- ☐ Provide reinforcement that is:
  - ☐ Immediate
  - ☐ Realistic
  - ☐ Valuable and meaningful
  - ☐ Safe and healthy
  - ☐ Appropriate in the current setting

- [ ] Provide praise that is:
  - [ ] Genuine
  - [ ] Specific
  - [ ] Public (when appropriate)
  - [ ] Loving, with touch (when appropriate)
- [ ] When planning a behavioral chart or contract:
  - [ ] Define the goal.
  - [ ] Break it down into manageable tasks.
- [ ] When creating a behavioral chart or contract:
  - [ ] Involve the child.
  - [ ] Validate his struggle.
  - [ ] Challenge him just enough.
  - [ ] Choose an appropriate reward.
- [ ] Be mindful of various factors when choosing an appropriate reward:
  - [ ] Context: is it developmentally appropriate?
  - [ ] Appropriateness: is the reward proportionate to the behavior?
  - [ ] Balance: is this overrewarding or creating a sense of entitlement?
  - [ ] Flexibility: is the reward still appealing or does it need to be changed after some time?
  - [ ] Current privileges: is there anything your child already gets that can be used as a reward?
- [ ] When implementing a behavioral chart or contract:
  - [ ] Show interest.
  - [ ] Encourage your child to maintain it and take responsibility.
  - [ ] Evaluate the behavioral chart or contract for effectiveness and adjust as necessary.

Strategies to Decrease Behavior (Chapter 7)

- [ ] Remember to use punishment sparingly and effectively.

☐ Enforce consequences that are:
  - ☐ Specific
  - ☐ Time-limited and finite
  - ☐ Meaningful
  - ☐ Appropriate
  - ☐ Closely related to the behavior
  - ☐ Require overcorrection (when appropriate).

☐ Follow through with consequences.

☐ Allow natural consequences to occur.

☐ When practicing extinction, consistently ignore the behavior even when it escalates (while ensuring that nobody gets hurt).

☐ Identify the causes of the child's behavior and practice satiation to prevent it from occurring.

Limit-Setting Skills **(Chapter 8)**

☐ Before setting limits, examine:
  - ☐ The purpose of setting this limit
  - ☐ Age-appropriateness and societal/cultural norms
  - ☐ Your child's capabilities
  - ☐ The parent/child relationship
  - ☐ Your emotional state
  - ☐ The number of limits already in place

☐ While communicating limits to the child:
  - ☐ Be mindful of the time and place.
  - ☐ Stay focused.
  - ☐ Stay calm.
  - ☐ Be clear and firm.
  - ☐ Be confident.
  - ☐ Communicate lovingly.
  - ☐ Follow through with the set limits.
  - ☐ Practice balancing consistency with flexibility when appropriate.

This is the end of *The Uncontrollable Child*. It isn't the end of your journey! This book has provided you with valuable skills, perspective-changing insights, and a framework in which to continue to learn, grow, and be the best parent that you can be. Remember that change is constant, and it is my greatest hope that *The Uncontrollable Child* remains with you as you navigate the ever-shifting landscape of your life.

Acknowledgments

First and foremost, I express my profound gratitude to the Almighty for granting me the ability to write this book and sending many wonderful individuals to turn my dream into a reality. Those individuals' names would fill another book; while I cannot mention everyone here, I thank you all from the bottom of my heart.

I'd like to publicly thank several of those special individuals:

My dear wife, Ruchama, an amazing partner and mother. I could have never accomplished this without your support and encouragement.

My incredible children, Michoel, Adina, Yisrael, Esti, Shua, and Shira, for teaching me how to be a better parent. Much of this book is credited to you.

My parents, for bringing me into this world, paving the road, and supporting me every step of the way.

Rabbi David Kleinkaufman, my teacher, mentor, and guide. You inspired this book and helped mold me into the person I am today.

Yael Dorfman, for transforming my words into a work of art. Your writing talents, patience, and dedication made working with you a true gift.

My New Harbinger team, Jess O'Brien, Clancy Drake, and Rona Bernstein, for an exceptional experience. I could not have been more pleased.

References

Alizadeh, S., M. B. Abu Talib, R. Abdullah, and M. Mansor. 2011. "Relationship between Parenting Style and Children's Behavior Problems." *Asian Social Science* 7, no.12: 195–200.

American Psychiatric Association. 2013. *Diagnostic and Statistical Manual of Mental Disorders, 5th ed.* Washington, DC: Author.

Baumeister, R. F., E. Bratlavsky, M. Muraven, and D. M. Tice. 1998. "Ego Depletion: Is the Active Self a Limited Resource?" *Journal of Personality and Social Psychology* 74, no. 5: 1252–65.

Baumrind, D. 1967. "Child Care Practices Anteceding Three Patterns of Preschool Behavior." *Genetic Psychology Monographs* 75, no. 1: 43–88.

Cameron, J., and W. D. Pierce. 1994. "Reinforcement, Reward and Intrinsic Motivation: A Meta-Analysis." *Review of Educational Research* 64: 363–423.

Deci E. L., and R. M. Ryan. 1985. *Intrinsic Motivation and Self-Determination in Human Behavior.* Boston: Springer.

Eisenberger, R., W. D. Pierce, and J. Cameron. 1999. "Effects of Reward on Intrinsic Motivation—Negative, Neutral, and Positive: Comment on Deci, Koestner, and Ryan (1999)." *Psychological Bulletin* 125, no. 6: 677–91.

Frey, B., and R. Jegen. 2000. "Motivation Crowding Theory: A Survey of Empirical Evidence." *Journal of Economic Surveys* 15.

Gagné, M., and E. Deci. 2005. "Self-Determination Theory and Work Motivation." *Journal of Organizational Behavior* 26, no. 4: 331–62.

Gershoff, E. T., J. E. Lansford, H. R. Sexton, P. Davis-Kean, and A. J. Sameroff. 2012. "Longitudinal Links Between Spanking and Children's Externalizing Behaviors in a National Sample of White, Black, Hispanic, and Asian American Families." *Child Development* 83, no. 3: 838–43.

Gottman, J. M., and R. W. Levenson. 2002. "A two-factor model for predicting when a couple will divorce: Exploratory analyses using 14-year longitudinal data." *Family Process* 41, 83–96.

Gottman, J. M., and N. Silver. 1999. *The Seven Principles for Making Marriage Work: A Practical Guide from the Country's Foremost Relationship Expert.* New York: Crown Publishing Group.

Jabeen, F., M. Anis-ul-Haque, and M. N. Riaz. 2013. "Parenting Styles as Predictors of Emotion Regulation Among Adolescents." *Pakistan Journal of Psychological Research* 28, no. 1: 85–105.

Jeannerod, M., and V. Frak. 1999. "Mental Imaging of Motor Activity in Humans." *Current Opinion in Neurobiology* 9: 735–39.

Kabat-Zinn, J., E. Wheeler, T. Light, A. Skillings, M. J. Scharf, T. G. Cropley, D. Hosmer, and J. D. Bernhard. 1998. "Influence of a Mindfulness Meditation-Based Stress Reduction Intervention on Rates of Skin Clearing in Patients with Moderate to Severe Psoriasis Undergoing Phototherapy (UVB) and Photochemotherapy (PUVA)." *Psychosomatic Medicine* 60, no. 5: 625–632.

Kohn, A. 1993. *Punished By Rewards: The Trouble with Gold Stars, Incentive Plans, A's, Praise, and Other Bribes.* New York: Houghton Mifflin.

Krasnegor, N. A., E. M. Blass, and M. A. Hofer (Eds.). 1987. *Perinatal Development: A Psychobiological Perspective.* Cambridge, MA: Academic Press.

Kübler-Ross, E. 1969. *On Death and Dying.* New York: Collier Books/ Macmillan.

Ledford, G. E. Jr., B. Gerhart, and M. Fang. 2013. "Negative Effects of Extrinsic Rewards on Intrinsic Motivation: More Smoke Than Fire." *WorldatWork Journal* 2013, no. 2: 17–29.

Lepper, M. R., D. Greene, and R. E. Nisbett. 1973. "Undermining Children's Intrinsic Interest with Extrinsic Reward: A Test of the 'Overjustification' Hypothesis." *Journal of Personality and Social Psychology* 28, no. 1: 129–37.

Linehan, M. M. 1993. *Cognitive-Behavioral Treatment of Borderline Personality Disorder.* New York: The Guilford Press.

Linehan, M. M. 2015. *DBT Skills Training Manual.* 2nd ed. New York: The Guilford Press.

Mendolia, M., and R. Kleck, 1993. "Effects of Talking About a Stressful Event on Arousal: Does What We Talk About Make a Difference?" *Journal of Personality and Social Psychology* 64, no. 2: 283–92.

Mittelstädt, V., and J. Miller. 2017. "Separating Limits on Preparation Versus Online Processing in Multitasking Paradigms: Evidence for Resource Models." *Journal of Experimental Psychology: Human Perception and Performance* 43, no. 1: 89–102.

National Institute of Mental Health. 2016. "Irritability in Children—Disruptive Mood Dysregulation Disorder." Accessed August 17, 2020. https://www.nimh.nih.gov/news/media/2016/irritability-in-children-disruptive-mood-dysregulation-disorder.shtml

Pink, D. H. 2009. *Drive: The Surprising Truth About What Motivates Us.* New York: Riverhead Books.

Piotrowski, J. T., M. A. Lapierre, and D. L. Linebarger. 2013. "Investigating Correlates of Self-Regulation in Early Childhood with a Representative Sample of English-Speaking American Families." *Journal of Child and Family Studies* 22, no. 3: 423–36.

Simons, D., and S. Wurtele. 2010. "Relationships Between Parents' Use of Corporal Punishment and Their Children's Endorsement of Spanking and Hitting Other Children." *Child Abuse & Neglect* 34: 639–46.

Skinner, B. F. 1953. *Science and Human Behavior.* New York: Macmillan.

Suomi, S. J. 2005. "Aggression and Social Behaviour in Rhesus Monkeys." *Novartis Foundation Symposia* 268: 216–253.

Taren, A. A., P. J. Gianaros, C. M. Greco, E. K. Linday, A. Fairgrieve, K. W. Brown, R. K. Rosen, et al. 2015. "Mindfulness Meditation Training Alters Stress-Related Amygdala Resting State Functional Connectivity: A Randomized Controlled Trial." *Social Cognitive and Affective Neuroscience* 10, no. 12: 1756–68.

Matis Miller, LCSW, is a licensed clinical social worker, and certified cognitive and dialectical behavior therapist with more than fifteen years of experience. He is founder, director, and supervisor of The Center for Cognitive & Behavioral Therapy of New Jersey. His educational and training background includes certification in cognitive behavioral therapy (CBT) from the Academy of Cognitive Therapy, and intensive training at the Beck Institute for Cognitive Behavioral Therapy. Miller has also been awarded certification from the DBT-Linehan Board of Certification in dialectical behavior therapy (DBT). He is a seasoned lecturer on CBT- and DBT-related topics—addressing parents, clients, and professionals—and is presently focused primarily on supervision, education, and consultations.

Foreword writer **Judith S. Beck, PhD,** is director of the Beck Institute for Cognitive Behavior Therapy, and past president of the Academy of Cognitive Therapy. Daughter of influential founder of cognitive therapy, Aaron T. Beck, Beck is author of *The Beck Diet Solution*.

Real change *is* possible

For more than forty-five years, New Harbinger has published proven-effective self-help books and pioneering workbooks to help readers of all ages and backgrounds improve mental health and well-being, and achieve lasting personal growth. In addition, our spirituality books offer profound guidance for deepening awareness and cultivating healing, self-discovery, and fulfillment.

Founded by psychologist Matthew McKay and Patrick Fanning, New Harbinger is proud to be an independent, employee-owned company. Our books reflect our core values of integrity, innovation, commitment, sustainability, compassion, and trust. Written by leaders in the field and recommended by therapists worldwide, New Harbinger books are practical, accessible, and provide real tools for real change.

 **newharbinger**publications

More ⏱ Instant Help Books for Teens

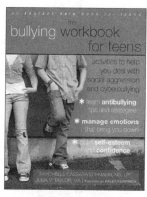

Register your **new harbinger** titles for additional benefits!

When you register your **new harbinger** title—purchased in any format, from any source—you get access to benefits like the following:

- Downloadable accessories like printable worksheets and extra content

- Instructional videos and audio files

- Information about updates, corrections, and new editions

Not every title has accessories, but we're adding new material all the time.

Access free accessories in 3 easy steps:

1. Sign in at NewHarbinger.com (or **register** to create an account).

2. Click on **register a book**. Search for your title and click the **register** button when it appears.

3. Click on the **book cover or title** to go to its details page. Click on **accessories** to view and access files.

That's all there is to it!

If you need help, visit:

NewHarbinger.com/accessories

new harbinger
CELEBRATING
40 YEARS